W9-DIS-788

Sales
Force
Automation

Sales
Force
Automation

Using the Latest Technology
to Make Your Sales Force
More Competitive

George W. Colombo

McGraw-Hill, Inc.

New York San Francisco Washington, D.C. Auckland Bogotá
Caracas Lisbon London Madrid Mexico City Milan
Montreal New Delhi San Juan Singapore
Sydney Tokyo Toronto

Library of Congress Cataloging-in-Publication Data

Colombo, George W.
   Sales force automation : using the latest technology to make your
sales force more competitive / George W. Colombo.
      p.   cm.
   Includes index.
   ISBN 0-07-011840-X
   1. Sales management—Data processing.   I. Title.
HF5438.4.C64   1994
658.8′1—dc20
                                                      93-32387
                                                      CIP

1 2 3 4 5 6 7 8 9 0   DOC/DOC   9 9 8 7 6 5 4 3

ISBN   0-07-011840-X

The sponsoring editor for this book was Philip Ruppel, the editing supervisor was
Frances Koblin, and the production supervisor was Suzanne W. Babeuf. It was set
in Baskerville by Calise Enterprises.

Printed and bound by R. R. Donnelley & Sons Company.

This book is printed on recycled, acid-free paper containing a minimum of 50% recycled de-inked fiber.

To Sandy

Contents

Foreword

Have you ever stood waist deep in the beautiful clear waters of the ocean and experienced the sensation of lurking unseen danger? Or perhaps you can imagine the fear that comes over you when you learn that a tsunami has been forecasted and is now racing at record speed toward your nice little beach cottage? I had sensations similar to these in the fall of 1990, but let me give you a little background on the events that brought me to that point.

I had just spent over nine years with GRiD computers, a company that produced the world's first and—at that time—most sophisticated laptop computer. GRiD also specialized in understanding and assisting customers with the whole range of issues related to field automation. That experience would serve me well in the coming months.

In 1990, I joined Storage Technology as Corporate Vice President, Americas Field Operations. Storage Technology manufactures, markets, and services information and storage retrieval devices for the large mainframe computers of major corporations around the world. Our mission is to establish long-term relationships with these corporations. Our customers depend upon us as their partner in managing sophisticated, enterprisewide information structures. We help our customers place their data on the right product, at the right time, and at the right price. As a result, not only are we selling hardware and software, but we are also providing professional and consulting services.

Storage Technology had just completed a five-year period of unbelievable growth after recovering from financial difficulties in the mid-1980s. The company's balance sheet was among the strongest in the industry. Its revenues had just topped $1 billion and were growing strongly. We were (and still are) widely recognized as the industry leader in providing storage solutions for large customers.

However, in 1990, Storage Technology was about to embark on a five-year plan that called for almost 100 percent growth in revenues as we prepared to deliver 14 major new products and services to our customers. I was excited about Storage Technology's growth potential and its strong leadership position in the market. But I knew that we did not have the resources in place to handle the kind of dramatic growth that we projected. I had the tsunami sensation in no uncertain terms!

I spent the next 90 days examining and measuring what we did have in place. What I found was both unnerving and exciting. Storage Technology's field force of over 2500 had been very successful over the previous five years, producing both record revenues and record profits for the company. However, the systems and processes that we were using had evolved from manually intensive systems that were over 20 years old! Those systems were actually preventing the sales team from being more productive. One alarming measurement showed that less than 40 percent of our top producers' time was being used for actual selling. The rest was taken up with backroom processes. While our systems might have been adequate for what we handled in the past, they certainly could not withstand the tsunami of growth that we would face in the coming years.

I saw that we needed new ways of doing business. I wanted to rip out the old processes and build a new structure from the ground up! And I knew that state-of-the-art technology would play a critical role in getting us to where we wanted to go.

With the help of teams in the field, we conducted an exhaustive review of all our existing processes. We identified 44 separate processes that would benefit from automation! In order to make this entire project easier to understand, and to help us establish appropriate expectations, we identified three general areas we wanted to address. Each of the processes would fall into one of these groupings. They were:

1. *Efficiency.* Those applications that could provide time savings when the salesman is away from the customer, thereby giving him more time to sell.

2. *Effectiveness.* Those applications that make the time in front of the customer more effective.

3. *Communications.* Those applications that allow easy transfer of information—usable information, not just data—between people and organizations.

We decided that our first priority would be to attack the efficiency issues because they would provide the largest measurable return on our investment.

Of course, I had to build a business case for our financial group. I did so, showing a very conservative (as it turns out) return on investment. I used only "hard" dollar savings in the justification, but outlined how the "soft" dollar savings could more than quadruple those savings realized from "hard" dollars.

In making our case, we examined the impact of technology, beginning with the basic computers that were available in the 1950s. We followed the evolution of automation from the plant, to the office, and finally to the latest technologies that were becoming available for workers based in the field.

The impact at every stage was positive, but financials (made possible by IBM and friends) documented a greater than 35 percent return on investment for the original automation.

Although the return on investment listed by various industry pundits showed that every new stage of automation in American industry had received a lower return on investment than had been achieved by the original automation, today, for the first time in over 30 years, companies were achieving close to that same return by using the technologies now available to automate the field force.

This kind of return on investment would make an exciting impact on any company, and Storage Technology executives were anxious to move forward. We got our budget.

Now, the task in front of us was to get ownership from a sales team that had been successful—very successful—for many years and might not readily see the need for a massive change in the way they did business.

I introduced the program, named *Apollo*, at our national sales meeting in the first quarter of 1991. I told our salespeople that I had been searching for a name that would simply and succinctly portray what we were doing. The most exciting interface of technology and human beings in my lifetime had been the Apollo moon missions in the 1960s. A relatively small group of individuals, narrowly focused on one objective, all sharing the same dream, using state-of-the-art technology, had placed a human being on the face of the moon. Our "moon shot" would transform us into the most productive sales and marketing organization in the world by employing the same model—a small group of individuals with a common dream, a narrow focus, using state-of-the-art technology.

I also pointed out that the original Apollo program took over 12 missions to achieve its goal. Likewise, Storage Technology's Apollo program would take as many missions. What our salespeople would see in 1991 was Apollo 1. Our five-year automation plan would get us to Apollo 12.

I wanted to set expectations and communicate a vision with this analogy. (A somewhat humorous side note: After this major presentation on the Apollo program, one young rep told me that he had been an avid follower of the Apollo program. He asked if I had realized that Apollo I was the mission that burned on the launch pad! When I heard that, I made up my mind to release Apollo 2 as soon as possible!)

We did not have internal resources that understood field automation, nor did we have any real experience in developing this type of software. I went outside the company for help. Apple Computer was the company that brought the most resources to the table. They were getting ready to introduce their new Powerbook line of laptop computers, and then were eager to provide us with their expertise in developing the software.

The management of the project was another area in which we went outside the company for help. I picked Anderson Consulting because of their unique understanding of the engineering of business processes, their expertise in the use of technology to support business needs, and their experience in change management (people issues). They also provided us with experience in designing the training curriculum and, of course, a thorough knowledge of field automation issues. One Storage Technology manager and I completed the team.

We had a tremendous advantage over most other companies that undertake this type of project, since I was the sole decision maker (versus the proverbial committee that can never decide) and was also able to draw on my 10 years of experience with GRiD doing this type of thing for other companies.

By early April 1991, we had set the middle of November as the target date for our first release of the software and training. I needed this unbelievably quick delivery because we were poised to launch a major new product in January 1992 and I wanted our people in the field to be literate on automation before we launched. Needless to say, all my partners were convinced that we would not make that date! In the end, not only did we meet the date, but we came in under budget and with software that was extremely rich in function. It was an absolutely superb effort on everyone's part.

The final key issue was training. We spent an extensive amount of time planning the training program with Anderson Consulting. We even piloted the training in much the same way as we had piloted the software or, for that matter, as we would pilot any new product. It worked extremely well. Our capture rate of the sales team, which we defined as the percentage of salespeople who readily took to using the system, was over 60 percent. That was a high figure, and was a direct result of the quality of our training process.

Finally, we established a help desk that was manned 16 hours a day. In addition to being a resource for salespeople in the field, we also used the help desk to gather statistics (who was calling and how often) and to measure the acceptance of the program, the use of various modules of the software, the reliability of the hardware and software, and the effectiveness of the training. We then used some of these statistics to determine our return on investment.

I want to make one important point about the initial introduction of Apollo. I knew from past experience how very important it was to quickly establish a beachhead for the project in the minds of the salespeople. The software had to be extremely intuitive, and it had to provide easy navigation from one module to another. We went to great lengths to ensure both of these points.

In addition, the entire project had to provide the return on investment that I had promised the board in order to get funding for the next five years of planned releases. We were diligent in measuring what we had been doing before introduction of Apollo, and made sure we had a methodology in place to collect measurements after introduction.

I also knew that the most dramatic returns would be measured by the productivity gains that occurred at the level of the individual sales rep. Therefore, all of our efforts during the first three releases targeted the sales rep and no other discipline in the organization.

This created some anger and frustration in some parts of the company, but it also ensured the success of the program. *We did not allow managers to have the system for the first six months.*

Apollo was to be perceived solely as a productivity system for the salespeople and not "Big Brother" trying to look over their shoulders or mandate any new management reports. My experience told me that this is a critical issue for the successful launch of any field automation project.

We are currently in the third release of Apollo. The two most recent releases have included presentation modules, product training modules, and new forecasting systems (our first management report). At every opportunity, we take time to reinforce our original vision to our people in the field, to reevaluate our priorities with them, and to set proper levels of expectation for everyone.

I am extremely proud of what our team has accomplished. We created what I believe is the finest field automation system in existence, and we did it on time and under budget. As I mentioned, we took many measurements on what we had done. The results at the end of the first year were almost frightening!

- The return on investment was less than eight months!
- Our customers' perception of our company had improved.
- The productivity of the sales team had increased by over 20 percent!
- Our cash-to-cash cycle was reduced by a week.
- The selling cycle was reduced 20 percent.
- With the use of computer-based training modules, we were able to reduce planned training costs by over $300,000 in one year!

Quite interestingly, we also discovered that something else had occurred: something that was exciting to all of us. In the process of all this, we had actually changed the culture of our field force from one that resisted change to one that not only welcomed change but actively pursued it!

We had reached the safety of the high ground that we had sought. We were now out of danger from the tsunami that was crashing on our shores.

JOHN WILLIAMS
Corporate Vice President
Storage Technology

Acknowledgments

Several individuals have made important contributions to this book. I would like to express my appreciation for the part each played in making this work possible.

Robert Faletra at *Computer Reseller News* and Richard March at *VARBusiness* gave me my first important forums as a writer in the computer industry.

It would be difficult to overstate my appreciation for Jeff Herman's professionalism, not to mention his skills, poise, and candor, as an agent. The support of Karen Hansen and Philip Ruppel, the editors at McGraw-Hill who immediately appreciated the importance of this topic, was pivotal in making this book a reality.

John Williams of Storage Technology, Professor Warren MacFarland of Harvard Business School, Al Smith of Saratoga Systems, Kevin Flynn of Apple Computer, and John Post of Hewlett-Packard's Medical Products Group were all early supporters of this book. They were unselfish with their time, allowing me to understand and benefit from their experience with and insight into the entire range of sales automation issues.

Throughout this project, Rich Bohn of the Denali Group was a tremendous resource, unfailingly generous with information, cooperation, and encouragement.

GEORGE W. COLOMBO

PART 1

The Sales Department of the Twenty-First Century

Introduction

In the old joke, when Tarzan returned home to Jane at the end of a particularly rough day, she asked him how his day went. He looked at her and replied, "Jane, it's a jungle out there!"

It is easy to have the same reaction when surveying the sales environment of the 1990s. In fact, I doubt that many analysts or observers would dispute the assertion that today's sales environment is more competitive than at any previous time. In industry after industry, as technology brings the nations of the world closer, businesses must be concerned with more competitors than ever before, both foreign and domestic. Moreover, the speed at which change is occurring in the marketplace is nothing short of breathtaking. For example, in the airline industry price wars that used to evolve over a period of weeks now take place not in days but in hours! In the computer industry, the entire life cycle of products has been compressed from approximately six years to six months or less!

To keep pace with the demands of this increasingly competitive environment, salespeople are being asked to become better and more productive at what they do, both quantitatively and qualitatively. In other words, they have to call on more customers and, at the same time, do a better job with each customer they call on. If nothing else had changed, the nature of the demands that are being made on the sales department would be impossible to achieve.

But, as so often happens, technology has come to the rescue. The technological revolution now going on in the sales department will give salespeople the tools to enhance sales productivity to a degree undreamed of just a short time ago. Collectively, this set of tools has come to be referred to as *sales force automation*.

In the following chapters, we will examine:

- What sales force automation is
- Why sales force automation is important
- How sales force automation benefits managers and salespeople

Before we begin, however, there are a few issues that I think need to be addressed. First, it is important to point out that sales force automation is not a technology that benefits only large companies. The fact of the matter is that this technology can improve any sales operation, even a single, independent salesperson. Along the same lines, it should be noted that sales force automation technology has become extremely affordable, well within the financial reach of any company or individual salesperson.

I would also like to address some of the oft-repeated criticisms of the concept of sales force automation. Certain writers and sales management consultants seem to dismiss the entire notion of sales force automation, almost out of hand. Jack Falvey, a well-known speaker and writer on sales management issues, is representative of this type of critic. In an article entitled "If Sales Force Automation Is the Answer, What's the Question?" in the December 1992 issue of *Sales & Marketing Management Magazine,* Jack raises some important points that deserve careful response. While all of these issues receive more extensive discussion elsewhere in this book, there are a few particulars that I would like to discuss here.

The basic question that sales force automation answers for sales managers is, "How can I increase profitability?" And, as we all know from our earliest business experiences, increased profitability results from enhanced sales productivity and/or meaningful cost reductions.

With regard to sales productivity, I believe that if sales force automation technology does not help your people sell more, then it is, indeed, a pointless undertaking. In contrast to the critics' assumptions, however, the facts indicate that tremendous increases in productivity are being achieved regularly. One of the companies that I studied for this book, Storage Technology Corporation, a $1.58 billion computer products manufacturer, projects a three-year revenue increase of between $13 million and $81 million attributable directly to their remarkable custom-designed, Macintosh-based sales force automation system. This type of result is not merely anecdotal; in fact, it corroborates other research in the field, going all the way back to the now famous article, "Automation to Boost Sales and Marketing," by Rowland Moriarty and Gordon Swartz in the January-February 1989 issue of *Harvard Business Review*.

Sales force automation is proving to be equally effective in helping to reduce costs. For example, Storage Technology was able to identify over $100,000 in savings that resulted solely from reducing the distribution of paper to the field offices!

Another point that Falvey makes in the *Sales & Marketing Management Magazine* article is that sales force automation technology cannot substitute for traditional sales skills. He writes:

> Soon, we're told, no sale will be made without a laptop or, at minimum, notebook computer present. These powerful tools of the future are supposedly the answer for all field sales force dilemmas. There does, however, seem to be one minor element missing in this premise: We have yet to come up with a set of questions adequate to this most eloquent of technological answers...Over the past 15 years, I've spent numerous days in the field with some of the best sales professionals in the world, and I've yet to see even one of them bring a computer into a sales call. Instead, they focus on their customers and on the objective of the call. They don't want anything to get in the way of what they're doing. To them, selling isn't an arcade game....With managers everywhere firmly entrenched in the information age, some are now waking up to the fact that having more information readily at hand doesn't really make us better managers...Again, there are few analytical problems that can't be solved just as easily by putting pencil to paper. (Reprinted by permission of *Sales & Marketing Management*. Copyright © December 1992.)

Here, I completely agree, as do almost all of the leaders in the field of sales force automation. The objective of sales force automation is not to substitute technology for the skills of a sales professional, but rather to put tools in that professional's hands which augment and enhance his or her skills. Just as lab tests are never a substitute for a doctor's examination and diagnosis, sales automation technology is most effective when it is placed at the service of a set of highly developed professional sales skills.

Finally, whereas Jack Falvey asserts in his article that information overload is a greater problem than lack of information, I contend that the sales manager's problem is too much raw data and not enough digestible information. Here sales force automation technology can benefit the sales manager by quickly and easily translating unfathomable amounts of raw data into understandable, useful information. The simple fact of the matter is that conducting an analysis of the sales data, by zip code, for three product lines over 18 months is far beyond the scope of what can be easily done by "putting pencil to paper." Without the intelligent application of technology, as the old New Englander once said, "You can't get there from here."

I think that the most succinct summation of the situation came during a discussion I had with Professor Warren MacFarland at Harvard Business School. Commenting on the role of technology in today's competitive sales and marketing environment, he said, "Sales force automation is no longer a competitive advantage; it is now a competitive necessity."

So, the real issue confronting sales managers today is not whether they ought to automate their sales efforts but what sales force automation is, what it does, and how to best go about the process of automating. My hope is that the book you are now holding in your hands will help you confront these issues.

As you read, you should not think of sales force automation as an end in itself. Instead, see it for what it really is—a powerful tool that, used properly, will help you achieve your sales and business objectives. Just as a hammer and chisel will not make you a great sculptor, sales force automation will not make you a great salesperson or a great sales manager, but as we navigate into the twenty-first century, an investment in sales force automation technology is becoming the ante that allows you to sit at the table where the high-stake games of business and sales are won and lost.

1
The Future of Sales Management

How Some Companies Are Already Using Sales Force Automation to Gain a Competitive Advantage

Steve is a Marketing Representative for Storage Technology Corporation. He is responsible for a sales territory in the metropolitan Boston area. Storage Technology manufactures, sells, and services storage and retrieval devices for mainframe and midrange computer systems, as well as enterprisewide computer networks. The products that Steve sells are big-ticket items that incorporate extremely sophisticated, state-of-the-art technology.

Steve left an important customer's office one morning with a problem. Steve and his customer had discussed a particular application for one of Storage Technology's products that was more involved than what was called for in the product's specifications. Steve's customer had a great deal of confidence in Storage Technology as a supplier, but was unsure of the product's ability to meet his requirements. Steve was asked to research the matter to try to find instances of other customers who were using that same product in a similar fashion.

When Steve got back to his office, he logged on to Storage Technology's electronic mail system, which gave him immediate access to every other Storage Technology salesperson across the country. In minutes, Steve sent several hundred salespeople an electronic message describing his customer's requirements and asking if there were any other customers using Storage Technology products in a similar manner.

By that same afternoon, Steve had the ammunition he needed. As it turned out, several large customers were using the Storage Technology product in precisely the same way that Steve's customer had considered using it. By the end of the business day, Steve's customer had a fax containing the names and phone numbers of five references. By the end of the week, Steve had landed the order.

Dave is a salesperson with ComputerLand, the world's largest retailer of desktop and portable computer systems. Computer-Land, like every other player in the brutally competitive computer business, must regularly address issues of price and availability.

On one recent sales call, a large insurance company asked Dave about the availability of Apple's latest PowerBook computer. Because of its tremendous popularity, demand for this particular model was far ahead of supply. Every Apple reseller was suffering from shortages as a result of limited availability from the manufacturer.

Dave carries a notebook computer with him on every sales call. When the customer indicated that his company was ready to purchase several dozen of the machines as soon as it could locate a supplier who had them in stock, Dave used his computer to call ComputerLand's distribution facility in Indianapolis. Dave was able to determine that ComputerLand did, indeed, have the scarce machines in stock. Upon the customer's approval, Dave was able to order the machines for his customer. Because of Dave's ability to respond immediately, he was able to secure the order on the spot. The machines were shipped from Computer-Land to the customer that same afternoon.

Both of these stories, of course, illustrate the use of computer technology to support and enhance the effectiveness of salespeople. Each company is using sales force automation as a competitive weapon in the marketplace. Each company is committed to a long-term, strategic plan that leverages the use of computer technology to support and enhance the sales function.

However, even among those companies that have adopted sales force automation technology effectively, there are some dramatic differences in how the issue of automation is approached and in the choices of specific tasks to automate. Before we continue, then, we will take some time to examine the range of functions that are available in sales force automation systems. Like ordering a meal at a fine restaurant, we need to closely examine our alternatives before making any final selection.

What Is Sales Force Automation Anyway?

No sales force automation system has every one of the options that I am going to describe in this section. In fact, after interviewing dozens of executives at companies that had successfully implemented some form of sales force automation, I did not find a single company that had automated every possible function. Instead, each successful company had automated selectively. This list of functions, then, is not meant to serve as a gauge against which to judge the completeness of your sales force automation project. Instead, it is here to give you a general sense of the range of functions that are available.

A useful way to think of sales force automation is in terms of these three broad areas of functionality:

1. Personal productivity
2. Communications
3. Transaction support and processing

Personal Productivity

The functions that fall into this category, as the name of the category implies, are those that allow a salesperson to work more productively. These functions include:

- Contact management
- Word processing
- Calendar management
- Automated sales plans, tactics, and ticklers
- Geographic information
- Computer-based presentations

Contact Management.   The most basic function in any sales force automation system is contact management. Contact management, in its simplest form, is like an electronic Rolodex listing of all the customer contacts that a salesperson makes in the course of conducting business. Like a manual system, an electronic contact file will include information like:

Last name
First name
Company
Address
Mailstop
Phone number
Fax number
Title

Depending on your business, there might be several additional items that you might want to track, perhaps dozens. These might be pieces of information that you consider important to know, but that could be unwieldy or impractical to track with a manual system.

Industry
Client, prospect, or suspect
Date of last order
Name of administrative assistant
Contact's birthday

Using a computer to track these items has several important advantages over trying to accomplish the same thing manually. First of all, it is easier to make changes, corrections, or updates. This is particularly true when those changes affect more than one contact. For example, if your largest account moves to a new location, it might be necessary to change the addresses of dozens of contacts within that company.

In addition, the computer gives you the capability of quickly searching through your contacts to find a particular contact or group of contacts. For instance, you might want to find only those contacts who have purchased products within the past six months and who live in Florida. While this information might exist somewhere in a manual system, there is no easy or convenient way to retrieve it. A sales force automation system will allow you to retrieve it easily.

Also, your contacts can be sorted according to any one of the pieces of information that you are tracking. You might need a client listing sorted by company name for a sales report, or a listing by zip code for mailing labels, or a list of all your clients with a birthday in March. Whatever your needs are, a sales force automation system will be able to accommodate them quickly and easily.

An important, closely related variation of contact management is account management. Contact management and account management are similar, but not exactly the same thing. The difference is orientation. Contact management uses the individual contact as the primary organizing unit. Account management considers the company to be the primary organizing unit, treating each individual contact as a subset of the company. There is no right or wrong approach, as we shall see in Chapter 3. Each approach can be useful, depending on your needs.

Word Processing.   Written communication plays a large part in the lives of most salespeople. Of primary importance, of course, is the need for written communication with customers. And, while the phone and the fax machine have assumed an important role in customer communications, there are still instances when there is no effective substitute for a letter. For example, in my career as a sales manager, one of my long-standing obsessions is with the idea of having salespeople send out thank-you letters immediately after an initial sales call. I believe that this seemingly insignificant gesture can often make the difference between a favorable impression or one that is not as favorable. Sometimes, it can make the difference between ultimate success and failure. But in spite of its potential impact, this simple task is usually neglected because there is no easy way for a salesperson to get it done. There always seem to be other, more pressing responsibilities that need attention. A sales force automation system can abbreviate the time it takes to accomplish this task to no more than a minute or two, the time it takes to execute a few keystrokes.

Many salespeople also find it useful to send form letters to groups of clients or prospects. A sales force automation system allows this to be done easily, merging client information that is recorded in the contact management section with a letter created in the word processing section. Also, for fliers or brochures that do not need to be "personalized," creating mailing labels becomes a simple matter.

Another important aspect of written communications is sales call reporting. The impact of sales force automation on call reporting will be discussed in detail in Chapter 3. For right now, though, we should merely note that sales force automation makes all of a salesperson's written communications easier and faster.

Calendar Management.   It may be trite, but it is nevertheless true, that time is the raw material out of which a salesperson's livelihood is fashioned. This simple truth is that if you were able to improve the time management skills of your salespeople—and nothing else—you would see a meaningful and measurable increase in their productivity. Electronic calendar management, as part of a sales force automation system, can make time management easier and less prone to errors or oversights.

When a salesperson schedules appointments, telephone calls, or to-do items on an electronic calendar, the system automatically checks for conflicts as appointments are scheduled, eliminating the need for rescheduling. An electronic calendar can assign a relative priority to each item. It can also create an electronic link between a scheduled event and a particular contact or account, so that the appointment or call information is not only accessible as part of the salesperson's calendar, but it is also accessible as part of the contact or account history. This makes the information contained in the calendar much more useful, since it can be viewed from a number of different perspectives.

For the sales manager, electronic calendar management automatically consolidates information concerning the whereabouts of the entire sales force. Salespeople no longer need to submit weekly or monthly calendars; instead, that information is automatically generated when salespeople schedule their appointments. The system also allows salespeople to instantly update their appointments and schedules from the field, so that the calendar the sales manager is working with is never outdated.

In addition to the month-at-a-glance view of activities and to-do items shown in Figure 1-1, a salesperson or manager can look at a day, a week, or an entire quarter. The underlying detail for each item is also immediately available, as shown in Figure 1-2.

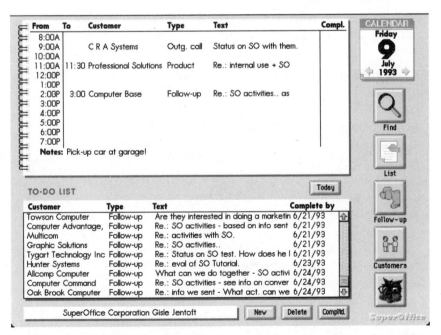

Figure 1-1. The Big Picture. Electronic calendar management allows salespeople to automatically schedule and update appointments and tasks. *(Courtesy of SuperOffice Corporation.)*

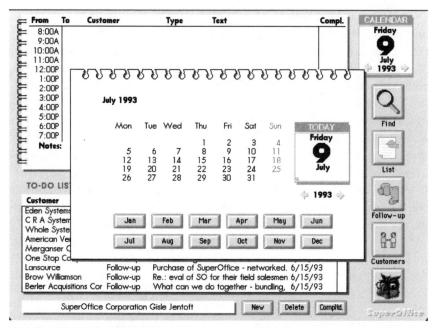

Figure 1-2. The Details. Using electronic calendar management, salespeople can access background information. *(Courtesy of SuperOffice Corporation.)*

Automated Sales Plans, Tactics, and Ticklers.

In many sales situations, it is possible to identify a certain sequence of events that ought to be followed. For example, after an initial sales call, you might want to have salespeople send out a thank-you letter immediately, and follow it up with a telephone call three days later. In the real world, it is often difficult for busy salespeople to keep track of these items. As a result, important follow-up items often get neglected. When this happens, a salesperson's diligent prospecting efforts become wasted and valuable prospects are squandered.

A sales force automation system can automatically remind a salesperson to send the thank-you letter and schedule the follow-up phone call as soon as the initial meeting is entered into the system. It can also notify the sales manger if these things are not done.

Another sales situation might call for a regular follow-up every year or two after the sale, depending on the "itch cycle" associated with your product. It is particularly easy for follow-up calls like this to get overlooked because of the long lead times involved. The problem becomes more apparent if the salesperson who made the original sale leaves the company or is promoted. When that happens, the customer often falls through the cracks and becomes an "orphan." Automated sales tactics and ticklers prevent this from happening.

In most companies, sales managers must manage the process of sales. The automation of sales plans and tactics makes the process more apparent for you and your salespeople. As a result, your job becomes easier.

Geographic Information Systems. The administration and management of sales territories presents a tremendous challenge, even to the most experienced sales managers. While you would like to have your salespeople feel that territory administration is done fairly and reasonably, the truth of the matter is that it is usually more of an art than a science. A geographic information system allows a salesperson or sales manager to view and manipulate customer and/or prospect information on an electronic map. Customer information can be accessed directly from contact-management data. Information on potential prospects can be entered into the system directly as it is captured, or the information can be purchased in bulk in computer format from third-party sources.

Once the information is plotted on a map, the administration of territories becomes immeasurably more accurate. The information can also be manipulated much more easily. In addition, this type of visual representation will often reveal buying patterns or trends that would not otherwise be apparent.

Salespeople can use geographic information systems in planning their sales calls to make the most efficient use of their time. Drive time is minimized when sales call planning is done with geographic considerations in mind. In Figure 1-3, a salesperson uses sales force automation to identify prospects and customers within a geographic area, allowing the salesperson to manage his or her travel time more effectively.

Computer-Based Presentations. If it is true that prospecting and sales planning are the steak, then sales presentations are the siz-

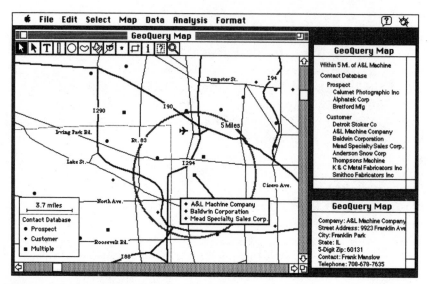

Figure 1-3. Managing Travel. Sales calls can be scheduled by sales automation software to minimize travel time. Here the salesperson identifies all prospects and customers within a five-mile radius. *(Courtesy of GeoQuery Corporation.)*

zle! When we think of champion salespeople, we naturally think of polished, professional sales presentations. And while it is true that prospecting and follow-up are the foundations of long-term sales success, it is also true that the moment of truth in front of a customer often comes when it is time for the salesperson to make the presentation. A compelling sales presentation can be the highly visible, dramatic climax of the long and arduous sales process that preceded it. Needless to say, the sales presentation deserves as much care, preparation, and pizazz as possible.

The computer can be a powerful presentation tool. With sales force automation dramatic and interactive computer-based presentations can be created easily and inexpensively. Moreover, once created, they can be easily customized for a particular customer or prospect or to take advantage of a particular sales opportunity.

Long-term sales success is not usually the result of pretty presentations, I will grant you. But a powerful, professional presentation can often be the tiebreaker in a close competitive situation.

Communications

As we move into the twenty-first century, it is clear that success in the marketplace is often determined by how quickly a company can deliver information to its customers and employees. Sales force automation systems address this issue in two ways.

1. Electronic mail
2. Fax capabilities and support

Electronic Mail.   When most sales mangers hear about electronic mail for the first time, it often does not strike them as particularly revolutionary or exciting. After all, in theory electronic mail does not create any tremendous new capabilities that did not exist with a manual system. Instead of sending letters or memos through the mail (or FedEx or intercompany mail), messages are sent electronically through a system that can deliver them immediately to any number of recipients. Certainly this is faster and easier than manual systems, but it isn't anything new, right?

The truth is that electronic mail is a transformational technology. It changes the very nature of communication and, as a result, can have a profound effect on corporate culture. As social scientists and historians have noted in other areas of communication and transportation, when the speed with which communication is accomplished is enhanced significantly, the very nature of the communication changes. Such is the power and effect of electronic mail.

If you truly want to keep your finger on the pulse of your sales force—and, by extension, if you truly want to stay close to your customers—then electronic mail can have a tremendous impact. Remarkably, this is as true in a sales environment where salespeople rarely leave the confines of the office as it is when they are based in the field.

Fax Capabilities and Support.   Next to the telephone, the fax machine is the most important piece of communication equipment in business. The widespread acceptance of fax technology is clear, and its usefulness is beyond question. In fact, most of us would find it difficult to imagine doing business without fax capability.

The field-based salesperson is, of course, at a disadvantage.

While it is true that portable fax machines exist, they are difficult for most businesses to cost justify for their salespeople. In addition, they are usually too cumbersome to be brought along on most business trips. As a result, salespeople who need to send or receive faxes from the road are forced to use public facilities, often at hotels. While this is a functional solution, it is seldom convenient. And it is often an uncomfortable solution when documents of a sensitive, confidential nature must be sent or received.

Notebook computers equipped with fax modems present a partial, if not ideal, solution. Fax machine images can be received directly on a notebook computer. The faxed document can be read and, if necessary, saved and printed out. Documents created on the computer can be sent directly to a fax machine without having first to be printed out. Although fax modems do not allow documents that were not created on the computer to be easily faxed, they represent a convenient, inexpensive way to handle the great majority of most of a salesperson's communications from the road.

Transaction Processing and Support

Obviously, the function of a salesperson is to secure and fulfill orders for products and services. This is not always as simple a process as it sounds. In fact, in many sales situations, when a customer agrees to order a product at a particular price, the process is just beginning. The following description may not represent your company's sales situation in every respect, but at least parts of it should be familiar to most salespeople and sales managers.

First, you need to find out if the products on your sales order are in stock and available for shipment. When appropriate, you must also determine if the order includes products that are incompatible or mutually exclusive. Then, you must get your customer's credit approved. Next, the sales order must be written up, sent to the home office, and entered into the company's system. Only after these steps are completed is it possible to tell a customer with any degree of certainty when the order might be shipped or received. If the delivery forecast is not acceptable to the customer, the entire order could be lost! (And you want to know why it is so difficult to keep good salespeople!)

A computer-based sales system can simplify and expedite all of these steps. It allows the salesperson to check the inventory status of items on a sales order and allocate the product in the warehouse for a customer via modem directly from the client's office. Your customer's credit status can be checked and the order can be approved for shipment instantly. The order can then be transmitted directly from the field to the company computer without having to be reentered. Finally, anticipated delivery can be estimated right on the spot. A process that once took place over a matter of days or weeks can now take place within hours or even minutes! (In Chapter 5, we shall look at the impact that this kind of speed can have on your business.)

It is often useful or necessary for a salesperson to have access to a customer's history. For example, a new buyer might not know what products were ordered in the past. Sometimes, having access to a customer's purchasing history will allow a salesperson to structure an order so that the customer can take advantage of a volume discount or promotional program. For many reasons, access to client history can often make the difference between successfully concluding a sales call and delivering superior customer service, or losing the momentum of the moment and needing to make a follow-up visit or phone call that may or may not be successful.

Computer technology is a tool that can eliminate the need for a salesperson having to return to the office to research and locate a customer's ordering history. Instead, with a sales force automation system, the salesperson will either have the necessary information instantly available on his or her notebook computer or be able to access it directly from a client's office via modem.

Electronic access to historical sales information can also be extremely useful to sales managers in the administration and analysis of sales territories. Most sales managers would agree that sales territory administration (and, as a result, quota assignments) is usually fairly subjective. A sales force automation system that allows you to access sales history, and then examine and manipulate that information, makes territory administration much more objective. As a result, you will be able to make better judgments about sales territories and, therefore, will need to

spend much less time explaining and justifying territory assignments.

Summary

Storage Technology and ComputerLand are examples of the
kinds of companies that are already using sales force automation
as a strategic competitive weapon. Any sales force, regardless of
its size, product, or structure, can use computer technology to
enhance its effectiveness.

Sales force automation encompasses a broad range of functions. It is neither necessary nor is it desirable for a sales manager
to attempt to automate every aspect of the sales process. Instead,
you should become familiar with the options, and look for the
areas in which you can leverage technology most effectively.

2
The Right Time for Sales Force Automation

If we survey this country's business landscape, it is clear that computer technology has had a profound impact on virtually every aspect of the American corporation—accounting, manufacturing, marketing, distribution, and operations. Only the sales department has remained stubbornly resistant to technology's productivity impact. While there are several reasons for this, which are discussed, it is important to realize that business and technological factors are converging to change the face of our sales operations forever.

Sales Department Resistance to Automation

It is not true that progressive managers have never tried to introduce computer technology to the sales department. But even when sales managers have attempted to automate their sales efforts, the results often left a great deal to be desired. I once spoke with the sales manager of a radio station in Florida whose station had made a substantial investment in notebook computers for all of its salespeople. These computers were used to connect the salespeople to the station's main computer system over telephone lines, allowing salespeople to provide their customers with instant information on the availability of commercial time slots. So far, so good. Later on in the conversation, though, I was amazed to discover that these same salespeople were still required to submit handwritten sales call reports, even though the station already had the capability to generate call reports automatically with the system. This is the rough equivalent of supplying the salespeople with company cars, then hitching a team of horses to the front bumper to get the cars to run!

There are several factors that, historically, have contributed to the slow implementation of computer technology by the sales department and the even slower acceptance of that technology by salespeople and sales managers. One significant factor is the notoriously independent nature of salespeople. Most sales managers realize that the qualities that allow salespeople to function well in the uncertain, competitive world of sales are the same qualities that make these salespeople difficult to manage. And while we sometimes wish that this independent nature could be turned on and off to suit our managerial requirements, the reality is that this is simply not possible.

As a sales manager, then, you should recognize that salespeople will not enthusiastically embrace a sales automation project just because you think that it is a good idea, or even because your company's upper management thinks that it is a good idea. In fact, it is more likely that salespeople will see a mandated automation project as an intrusion of "big brother" into their lives, a control mechanism to be ignored, resisted, or, if necessary, actively undermined. In fact, many sales managers who tried to implement sales force automation systems have found themselves being confronted by salespeople with the ultimatum, "Do you want me to spend time fooling around with this stuff, or do you want me out there selling?" The sales manager's typical response to that question explains why so much of the money and effort spent on sales automation projects have been wasted or misguided.

> When we got our sales force automation project started, I refused to give it to my managers for the first six months of the project. I wanted the salesmen to feel it was a productivity tool for them, that it wasn't big brother creating more reports, big brother coming down into their territories to find out what they were doing. We were really sensitive to the sales people on that issue.
>
> JOHN WILLIAMS
> *Storage Technology*

Another reason that sales departments have been so slow to automate has to do with the fact that there are so many different ways to sell. In contrast, when a company automates its accounting system, there is generally a finite number of variables that need to be addressed. Most accounting is fairly standard and can be automated within the confines of a somewhat narrow range of alternatives. The same is also true for other, more specialized applications. One doctor's office runs pretty much like another's (or like a chiropractor's or a veterinarian's, for that matter).

But the sales department is something else entirely. Consider the differences between the jobs of a sales representative for a distributor of musical instruments and a sales representative for a life insurance company. Other than the fact that both salespeople function in a commission-based environment, there are more differences than similarities in their day-to-day activities.

Even within the same industry, each company's sales department seems to have its own style, its own methods, and its own flow. In fact, every sales operation has its own "fingerprint." This being the case, it has been difficult to find a standard approach to sales automation that does not require a company to change the way it does business in order to conform to the system's requirements. Thankfully, as we shall see later, this is not necessary.

Finally, in attempting to meet the needs of a sales force that is based in the field, there have been significant logistical and technological challenges that needed to be overcome. Although office-based sales efforts—telemarketing, for example—have been successfully automated for quite some time, the "road warrior" has not yet been able to enjoy the benefits of automation. One area of technical challenge has been to find the best way to move information from the home office to the field or from the field to the home office. Ensuring the security of data is another example of a technical challenge that needed to be met before salespeople could be computerized. But, as we will see in a moment, recent technical innovations in both hardware and software have now made it possible to extend the benefits of automation to the salesperson in the field.

The Impact of Rapidly Developing Technologies

It is clear to even a casual observer that the rate at which technology is advancing is breathtaking. These advances in computer and communications technology are accelerating the trend towards automating the sales force. In fact, these developments are taking place so rapidly that any discussion of them runs the risk of being outdated by the time it reaches print.

The timeliness of adopting notebook technology to automate sales forces could not be better than right now. There is a convergence of several different technologies that is making the use of notebook computers by sales reps much more productive. One important factor is the greatly improved communications links between notebooks and networks, as well as between networks and corporate mainframes. Communications software is more mature, is easier to use, and is more reliable. Also, faster modems allow for the transfer of larger amounts of data between notebook computers in the field and the home office. As all of these factors converge, we can arm the sales person with better information in order to get them out of the information hassle business and get them into the business of increasing sales and customer satisfaction.

ED ANDERSON
ComputerLand Corporation

The areas in which technological advances are affecting the automation of the sales force can be grouped into four main categories. They are:

1. Notebook computer technology
2. Sales force automation software
3. Communications technology
4. Network technology

Notebook Computer Technology

Less than 10 years ago, the idea of a full-featured, full-powered, battery-operated computer was a fantasy that was more likely to be discussed in the pages of a science fiction magazine than in a serious business publication. Today, you only have to walk down the aisle of any cross-country flight to see exactly how ubiquitous this technology has become. Notebook computers are commonplace, a standard accessory in the briefcase of today's mobile business professional.

Sales statistics from the computer industry support this observation. Since 1989, notebook computers have been the fastest growing segment of computer sales, commanding an ever-increasing share of the overall microcomputer market. Most industry observers point to two factors that are driving this trend. First of all, the price of these systems has declined dramatically. While it is true that the price of all computer technology has plummeted, the prices of laptop and notebook systems have declined even more rapidly than the prices of desktop systems.

Much more important, though, is the fact that the power of these notebook computers has increased to the extent that they are every bit as capable and powerful as their desktop counterparts. Today's notebook computers have enough computing horsepower to function as primary computers, rather than as expensive peripheral devices to be used in conjunction with a desktop system.

Not only are the memory, processing power, and storage capabilities of notebook computers fully equivalent to desktop systems, but now notebook systems are increasingly likely to be equipped with vivid, full-color display screens, eliminating the last consequential distinction. As a result, when sales managers consider making an investment in computer systems for the sales force, they need no longer weigh the trade-off between the power of desktop systems and the convenience and portability of notebook systems.

And while the capability of these systems is increasing, their size and weight is decreasing. Today's average notebook system weighs about six pounds, and some weigh much less. All can easily fit inside a standard briefcase. They are small enough to be used comfortably on an airplane or in an automobile. In fact, usability factors, rather than miniaturization technology, are preventing systems from getting any smaller. If notebook computers became much smaller than they are today, their keyboards and screens would be too small to be truly useful.

There is every indication that the trend toward notebook computers and away from desktop computers will accelerate in the years to come. Manufacturers of notebook computers are putting the last piece of the puzzle in place with the advent of *docking stations* for notebook computers (see Figure 2-1). As the state of the art of notebook technology has progressed, the last remaining objection to using a notebook computer as a primary system has been the fact that, when people return to the office from the road, they often prefer to work with a larger keyboard and monitor than they have on their notebooks. Also, they often need greater storage capacity and the ability to conveniently back up their data. Finally, they often need to connect to a company network or mainframe.

All of these things have long been possible with notebook computers, but the process was cumbersome and inconvenient. It usually involved connecting several cables to the back of the computer upon arriving back at the office, and then unconnecting them when leaving. With a docking station, when a salesperson returns to the office, the notebook computer is slipped inside the docking station, which may have additional storage, a full-size keyboard, and a full-size monitor attached, as well as all the necessary network connections. When it is time to leave the office, the notebook computer is simply removed and is immediately ready to go. As docking stations become more functional and less

Figure 2-1. Docking Station. When a salesperson returns to the office, his or her notebook computer can instantly acquire the functionality of a full-featured desktop machine through the use of docking station technology. *(Courtesy of Apple Computers, Inc. John Greenleigh, photographer.)*

expensive, some visionaries are projecting a time when notebook computers command the largest share of the computer market, while desktop systems become specialized, niche products for particular applications.

In whatever way this scenario ultimately unfolds, the important point is this: notebook computers are more capable and less expensive than ever before. As a result, the feasibility of equipping a sales force with notebook computers has increased dramatically over the last five years in terms of cost and functionality.

Sales Force Automation Software

If the advances that have been made in notebook computer technology represent an evolutionary change, then it would be accurate to say that the advances in the quality, capability, and cost effectiveness of sales force automation software have been nothing short of revolutionary. And, as is always the case, it is the quality of the software that dictates the acceptance of computer technology in a market.

Five years ago, sales force automation software barely existed as a distinct software category. What did exist could be charitably described as "roll your own." In fact, many of the software offerings were products that were developed by salespeople for their own use. Only as an afterthought were these products marketed to the general public. The first sales force automation applications were crude and tended to consist primarily of contact management and word processing. But, as notebook computer technology evolved to a point that made mobile computing truly practical, software developers began to pay serious attention to meeting the needs of field-based salespeople.

> Sales automation is a fact of life. It is a fait accompli. The companies who are making it, who are growing, are the ones who are taking full advantage of the computer. Those that are failing are still in the paper and pencil stage.
>
> DAVID JOY
> *Stanley Tools*

While contact management remains at the heart of sales force automation, the range of supporting functions, as we saw in Chapter 1, has grown dramatically. The software packages that are available on the market for sales force automation are extremely capable and sophisticated.

More important, though, is that today's software is much more user friendly than in the past; it is easy to use and intuitive. The importance of these qualities cannot be overemphasized. As we have already seen, salespeople do not gravitate easily toward computer technology. In Chapter 13, we explore several ways in which you can facilitate the acceptance of sales automation by your salespeople, but for right now, we should merely note that the ease of use of the software is a critically important factor in the success of any sales force automation undertaking. And today's software is easier to use than ever before.

Finally, there is the issue of supporting salespeople in the field. As organizations downsize, it is increasingly common to find not only salespeople but also their sales managers based in the field rather than at headquarters. A field-based manager needs to have a customer file that is a subset of the home office master customer file. It should include the account information of all his or her salespeople. How can a company provide the salespeople with the customer information they need (and, for the sake of security, not any more than they need), the sales manager with the customer and sales reporting information that he or she needs, and still maintain an up-to-date master customer file at headquarters? What if simultaneous changes are made to a customer's record in the field and at headquarters? How do both sets of changes get resolved? Up until recently, the technical challenge of addressing these issues proved to be an almost insurmountable obstacle. However, recent innovations in what the computer industry refers to as *distributed data base technology* have made it possible to provide practical solutions to these problems.

Communications Technology

Connections between computers are made over telephone lines through the use of modems. For the foreseeable future, telephone lines will provide the most important connection between salespeople and sales managers in the field and in the home office. (We look at other possibilities for the future in Chapter 14.) Historically, users have had to choose between modems that were painfully slow, but affordable, and those that were adequately fast, but prohibitively expensive.

Fortunately, the same factors that have driven computer prices down over the last several years have done the same thing to the prices of high-speed modems. As a result, it is now possible for salespeople in the field to communicate with the home office at a speed that makes such a hook up functional and cost effective.

I think salespeople thought they were automated back in the late 1970s when they got Hewlett-Packard financial calculators. That was a big step at the time. But true sales force automation was impossible until the technology became available to move enormous amounts of information out into the field, into the hands of the salespeople and, by extension, into the hands of the customers.

JOHN WILLIAMS
Storage Technology

Network Technology

All major sales force automation solutions involve sharing information among various people and departments within a company on a local area network. Many of the benefits of sales force automation come from being able to deliver information to the right people in an organization in a timely and useful manner. This is accomplished through the communications capabilities that a local area network provides.

As we mentioned earlier, the automation of office-based telemarketing operations is a relatively simple undertaking because of the ease with which an office-based user can be physically attached to a network. Connecting a field-based salesperson to a local area network is somewhat more complex. The objective is to allow a salesperson to log on to the network from a customer's office or from a hotel room and have access to all the network's data and services.

Recent advances in network software have allowed for tremendous improvements to be made in this area. Apple Computer, for example, distributes software called *AppleTalk Remote Access,* which allows a notebook computer in the field to log on to a network in the home office in a way that is identical in almost every respect with what the user would experience if he or she were actually sitting in the office.

Changes in Corporate America Make Sales Force Automation a Necessity

If recent technological advances have made sales force automation practical, then the evolution of the business climate in America over the last decade has made it a necessity. Professor Warren MacFarland of the Harvard Business School described the situation succinctly and accurately when he said, "In five years, there will be two types of companies: those that use the computer as a sales and marketing tool, and those that face bankruptcy." Without a doubt, Professor MacFarland is correct. Three distinct factors have combined to make this so: (1) increased emphasis on cost containment, (2) increased emphasis on customer satisfaction, and (3) the premium for speed.

Increased Emphasis on Cost Containment

Companies representing virtually every aspect of American business have found themselves experiencing a steady erosion of gross profit margins over the last decade. This is due to increased competitive pressures combined with significant shifts in consumer buying patterns. "Value buying" has undoubtedly become a permanent characteristic of the American consumer. The erosion of profit margins has, in turn, led management to undertake an increasingly intense scrutiny of all costs in order to remain competitive, including the costs associated with the sales department.

One of the consequences of cost containment measures is that sales organizations find themselves with a far smaller sales support structure than they had before. Therefore, salespeople and sales managers are increasingly finding it necessary to function without a secretary or administrative assistant for the sales department. Where such an individual was once available to handle duties such as routine correspondence, those responsibilities now fall to the salespeople and sales managers themselves. But while the administrative duties of the average salesperson have increased, there has been no commensurate decrease in sales quota to compensate for the time that can no longer be devoted to pure selling. In fact, we expect our salespeople to be more productive than ever before.

> There are a great deal fewer support people than there used to be. All the secretaries and administrative people are gone. The pressure is on. And since you don't have the legions of support people that you use to have, a lot of administrative functions have been delegated to salespeople who did not do them before.
>
> AL SMITH
> *Saratoga Systems*

Sales managers must also adjust to organizational structures that are generally flatter than they once were. This means that many managers have responsibility for 20 to 30 percent more salespeople than they had 10 years ago. (Chapter 9 discusses how sales force automation allows sales managers to painlessly eliminate many unnecessary costs from their operations.)

Increased Emphasis on Customer Satisfaction

Few veteran sales managers would dispute the fact that today's business climate places a far greater emphasis on customer satisfaction than it did a decade ago. In fact, customer satisfaction, in conjunction with the dynamic of staying close to the customer, is viewed by most organizations as a key strategic component of their sales and marketing plan. While a comprehensive discussion of this trend is beyond the scope of this book, and has, in fact, been done elsewhere, I will merely note that I believe that this is a healthy and appropriate direction for every business.

Since most businesses are paying at least lip service to customer satisfaction, the real differentiation in the marketplace will come from superior execution. We can see that the competitive bar in the area of customer satisfaction has been raised to a level that is higher than it has ever been before, and it is certain to get higher still. The competitive reality of the 1990s is that customers have choices. They expect a far greater degree of service than they ever did before and, as a result, are less tolerant of mistakes. If we allow things to slip through the cracks, our customers are more than willing to take their business elsewhere. Chapter 4 illustrates the ways in which computer technology helps salespeople deliver flawless customer service that will ensure superior customer satisfaction.

Premium for Speed

A final factor that is driving the trend towards automating the sales department is the extent to which speed has become a strategic advantage in the selling process. Once, it was acceptable for salespeople to promise to get back to customers with answers to questions. Increasingly, those salespeople are finding that by the time they get back to their customers with the necessary information, the sales opportunity has evaporated. The ability to respond to customers quickly is crucial to success, and the tolerances are narrower than ever before.

The issue of speed is critical in the marketplace. If you have to shuffle an order back and forth between the field and the home office before you can fulfill it, your customer is going to go somewhere else.

BRAD BARNES
McDonnell Douglas Helicopter

Similarly, the ability to compress the sales order cycle is becoming an extremely significant factor in a competitive situation. Your customers, who are under the same competitive pressures as you, are placing more and more emphasis on increased cash flow and reduced inventories. Reducing your sales order cycle from four days to two can make an important and measurable difference, certainly enough of a difference to determine whether or not you get the order. In Chapter 5, we see that the strategic use of computer technology in the sales department can make a dramatic difference.

Summary

While many sales operations have been slow to embrace computer technology, there are important factors affecting the business environment that are moving sales force automation from the category of being a competitive advantage to being a competitive necessity. At the same time, technological advances are making it easier, more functional, and less expensive than ever before for sales managers to implement sales force automation solutions.

Putting an intelligent device in the hands of a salesperson is extremely important. Allowing that individual to receive messages over a network, to send information back up to management, and giving the salesperson the ability to keep track of sales calls, to quickly receive data on sales efficiency, to immediately price out the total value of an order—all of these are critical issues. We have answered the question of whether or not the technology belongs in the hands of the field sales force. That was an issue four years ago and that issue has simply ended.

WARREN MACFARLAND
Harvard Business School

PART 2

Giving Salespeople a Winning Edge

3

Automation Enhances Sales Productivity

Most sales managers spend a great deal of time, as well as large amounts of money, in the pursuit of quality salespeople. It is not difficult to understand why. As Tom Peters reminds us, sales is, after all, where the money comes from.

Salespeople are responsible for the prospecting efforts that identify potential customers. Quality salespeople can then transform qualified prospects into profitable customers for your products. And, of course, salespeople shoulder the ongoing responsibility for the subsequent care for those customers and the maintenance of their long-term relationship with your company.

Your Salespeople Should Be Selling!

Simply put, as a sales manager, you want your salespeople to spend their time with customers, or, at least, on issues that directly relate to customers. The two primary areas of responsibility for salespeople are:

1. To generate revenue
2. To preserve, nurture, and protect the company's relationships with its customers

When we require that our salespeople spend significant amounts of time on activities that are not specifically productive in one of these two areas, then we, as sales managers, are not utilizing them properly. Today's business climate does not allow us the luxury of misusing or underutilizing a resource as valuable as sales talent.

A cursory review of most sales departments, however, reveals that underutilization is the rule rather than the exception. In fact, at a time when most businesses can least afford it, the situation is getting worse instead of better. Cost cutting has reduced or, in some cases, eliminated the support staff on which many sales departments relied for administrative and clerical help in the past. With the sales department secretaries gone, salespeople must find other ways to accomplish the routine administrative tasks that support the sales function. These tasks include:

- Generating thank-you letters
- Checking on sales order status for customers
- Determining product availability
- Entering sales orders
- Writing up proposals

In most companies, some or all of these tasks must now be accomplished by the salespeople themselves. While this may seem to be a reasonable solution to the problem, I believe that an extremely persuasive case can be made that it is not one that is in the best interest of the companies that adopt it.

First of all, salespeople are productive when they are in front of customers, not when they are in front of a keyboard. Being in front of customers is what we pay them to do. Every hour that one of your salespeople spends on administrative tasks is an hour that he or she is not spending selling your product in front of a prospect or customer. The typical rejoinder made by hard-line sales managers to this observation is that salespeople should be taking care of their administrative responsibilities on their own time and during nonselling hours. In a perfect world, that might work, but in the real world, the stark reality is quite a different thing indeed. The fact of the matter is that administrative and clerical tasks invariably take time away from selling.

> We did a productivity study of the sales force. We found that our salespeople were working hard, but they were encumbered with about 20 years of bureaucracy that had bogged them down. And I found out that only about 36 percent of their time on average was available for selling. The rest of it was backroom support and administration of the territory. My definition of selling is direct, face-to-face contact with a customer. And so, as far as I was concerned, that figure was way too low.
>
> JOHN WILLIAMS
> *Storage Technology*

Secondly, salespeople tend not to be particularly gifted in performing administrative tasks. Their interests and aptitudes lie elsewhere. At the risk of generalizing, I think most sales managers would agree with me that salespeople are usually not inclined to devote attention to the detail that administrative work often requires. The result is that sales orders get filled out incorrectly, letters get sent out with incorrect grammar and misspellings, or customers are forced to wait days before they can find out about the status of their orders. In each case, your company does not perform as well for its customers as it must in order to survive in a highly competitive environment.

A more serious risk created by assigning administrative tasks to salespeople is that they simply do not get done. Of course, sales orders will get written up, no matter what. But I can state without any fear of contradiction that most other administrative tasks, like sending thank-you letters, are not very high on the priority lists of most salespeople.

While this is understandable, it is also dangerous. The failure by salespeople to attend to details reflects poorly on a company that is looking to make a statement about customer service. On a more positive note, when a company pays attention to this type of detail, it sends a subtle but powerful message to its customers about its commitment to providing customer service.

Finally, many salespeople, when forced to devote too much of their time to administrative support tasks, look elsewhere for a job that allows them to spend their time selling. Salespeople are generally motivated by money. They will usually try to identify and associate with the work environment in which they can be most productive.

The plight that you face as a sales manager is obvious. The pressure to keep costs down does not allow you the luxury of maintaining a staff to attend to the administrative support of your salespeople. On the other hand, for a variety of reasons, your salespeople are not well suited to take care of their own administrative support functions. Sales force automation technology provides you with the answer to this dilemma. A sales force automation system will enable your salespeople to:

- Streamline the selling process
- Make prospecting and contact management more efficient
- Eliminate administrative time wasters
- Make sales calls more effective

Streamline the Selling Process

One way that a well-designed sales force automation system can make your salespeople more effective is by taking certain administrative tasks that had previously been handled separately from the sales process and building them right into the sales call. In doing so, these tasks can be accomplished more accurately, more elegantly, and at a lower cost than before.

Proposal Generation

Consider, as an example, the creation of product proposals for customers. Traditionally, certain high-ticket or sophisticated products are sold through a process that requires the salesperson to interview a prospect to ascertain the prospect's needs and to develop a context in which those needs can be addressed through the salesperson's products or services. When the salesperson has accomplished this, he beats a hasty retreat back to the office to generate a written proposal that reflects the prospect's specific needs. The proposal is then delivered or mailed to the prospect who is, no doubt, soliciting similar proposals for competitive products or services.

Some companies have used sales force automation to truncate this process and to short-circuit competitors at the same time. These companies use intelligent proposal generators that allow the salesperson to create proposals for clients during the course of an interview and to deliver those proposals on the spot.

It can sometimes be remarkable to see the system in operation. There have been instances when one of our salespeople is with a customer in a competitive situation. Now, of course, this is a situation where we have a relationship with the customer, not a cold call. While the customer is talking to us, our salesperson will finish up the details we need for a configuration, will hit a button and put the configuration in the proposal generation module, and deliver a hard copy to the customer while we are sitting there. And when we walk out of the office, the customer already has a proposal from us while our competition is still sitting in the lobby.

JOHN WILLIAMS
Storage Technology

Under the right circumstances, this approach has several advantages. First of all, it can cut several days out of the proposal process. This can be particularly valuable for the salesperson who is attempting to convey a sense of immediacy or urgency. (And, really, shouldn't all salespeople be attempting to do that?)

Along the same lines, the immediate delivery of a proposal allows the salesperson to maintain momentum in the sales situation, momentum that might otherwise be lost during the time that it takes to create and deliver a sales proposal. How many times have you seen an ostensibly hot prospect cool off during the time that it took for your salesperson to put their proposal together?

As an added benefit, this creates a favorable comparison for your company next to the competitor who takes two or three days to do what your salesperson was able to do on the spot. And occasionally this kind of immediacy will allow your salesperson to do an end run around the competition, closing the sale before the competition even has a chance to deliver a proposal!

The real point to all of this, though, is that automation allows a salesperson to create proposals more quickly and at a lower cost than they can be created otherwise. Moreover, it does so in a way that does not cut into your salesperson's valuable selling time.

Product Configuration

In addition to proposal generation, a sales force automation system can also help your salespeople to put together complex product configurations more accurately. Industries that sell technically sophisticated products such as computers or aircraft often require a salesperson to fill out a customer's order by choosing among several options. Sometimes these options are mutually exclusive; other times, one option will require that another be added in order for the first to function properly.

In these types of situations, product configuration can often take up a great deal of a salesperson's time. Moreover, some companies also require a sales manager to double-check sales orders before they are logged, so that configuration mistakes can be avoided.

We gave our salespeople a pricing tool that is incredibly slick. If the salesperson enters a product number, the system can tell the customer all about the product—the price, the features, everything. Also, it won't allow the salesperson to put incompatible products together. The salesperson can adjust the discount level, set up maintenance agreements, set up a service schedule, all right there in front of the customer.

JOHN WILLIAMS
Storage Technology

An intelligent configuration system will not allow a salesperson to create a sales order that is incomplete or incorrectly configured. Such a system will not accept product options that cannot work together or will not fit with each other. It will also automatically include any options that are necessary in order for the system or product to work properly.

> The system will not allow the salesperson to put a helicopter together that has incompatible parts, or mutually exclusive options. There is intelligence built into the system that will not allow it.
>
> BRAD BARNES
> *McDonnell Douglas Helicopter*

With an intelligent configuration system, you and your salespeople can save significant amounts of time that would otherwise need to be spent on product or system configuration. This translates, of course, into more time that can be spent by your salespeople in front of customers, selling your products and services.

Sales Order Generation

In some industries, the sales process is somewhat less sophisticated than what is found in a high-tech, high-ticket environment. Even in these situations, automation technology can significantly improve the process.

> Our sales automation system made our retail division salespeople much more efficient since they did not have to waste time adding up their orders, writing in product descriptions, calculating line item extensions, things like that. The system does all of this for them. And it not only made our people much more efficient, but it also made them a lot happier because they did not have to do all the grunt work that was involved in writing out orders.
>
> DAVID JOY
> *Stanley Tools*

A computer-based sales order system can replace the traditional three-part handwritten order form. When this happens, the sales order process becomes faster and more accurate. The sales orders themselves, now printed by machine instead of being written by hand, become easier for everyone to read, eliminating mistakes and misunderstandings. Also, the process of creating the sales order is shortened considerably, since the salesperson no longer has to do the math or write in product descriptions. The salesperson is free to devote more attention to the customer, and not forced to concentrate on the minutia that accompanies the process of writing up an order.

Make Prospecting and Contact Management More Efficient

For most salespeople, productivity is determined by this formula:

- Continuously prospect in order to identify potential customers
- Manage a large number of prospects efficiently over a period of time

The first part of the formula is clear. In virtually every type of sales situation, the larger a salesperson's active prospecting base is, the more successful that salesperson is going to be. Of course, more skilled salespeople will be more successful than less skilled salespeople, but at any skill level, the salesperson with the larger base of prospects is going to win.

The second part of the formula means that prospects must be cultivated and maintained until they are ready to buy, sometimes over a long period of time. For example, a prospect that one of your salespeople identifies might have just purchased a competitor's product and will not be ready to purchase again for another year or so. This individual, who might be an excellent prospect in every other respect, is simply not ready to buy right now. Rather than waste the prospecting effort that uncovered this potential customer, you will want your salesperson to maintain a tickler file that will allow him or her to contact this individual again at a later, more appropriate time.

> The clients that I have worked with that are using sales force
> automation technology are reporting dramatic improvements in
> sales—even in recession-impacted markets. They are reporting
> that sales are going up while sales head count is going down.
>
> GIL CARGILL
> *IDK Group*

Sales force automation will enhance the effectiveness of your
salespeople at both ends of the formula. At the front end,
automation technology can dramatically enhance a salesperson's
prospecting efforts. Prospecting lists can be purchased from a
variety of sources in a format that can be read directly into a
computer. This means that salespeople will no longer have to
work from printouts, but will, instead, have their raw prospecting
data in a form in which it is instantly usable. In addition, electronic mail and other electronic communications media allow
you to get leads that have been obtained from other sources into
the hands of your salespeople while those leads are still hot.

> My goal is to get a hot lead into the field the same day that I
> receive it. And to make sure that it gets into the hands of the
> right person. Once a salesperson looks at the date and sees
> that it came in three weeks ago, they figure that it is probably
> too late.
>
> JOHN POST
> *Hewlett-Packard*

Sales force automation is also an extremely effective tool at the
other end of the prospecting formula. Most products can be
characterized by what sales professionals refer to as an "itch
cycle." In other words, there is a certain predictable amount of
time that elapses between when a customer purchases a product
or service and when that customer is ready to purchase that product or service again. The itch cycle for automobiles is generally
around three to five years. For computers, it is somewhat shorter;
for industrial equipment, a little longer. Salespeople cannot

count on being lucky enough to identify and contact a potential customer at exactly the right time in the customer's itch cycle. If a customer is not ready to buy, it does not mean that the customer is not a good prospect; it merely means that the customer has been contacted prematurely in the itch cycle.

> The system has allowed us to take certain management and marketing guidelines and build them right into the system. As a result, the salespeople can focus more on selling and less on all the other peripheral stuff. That is the biggest impact that I see.
>
> SAM STEINHOUSE
> *Progressive Companies*

If your salespeople are prospecting properly, they will frequently identify customers who are otherwise qualified to buy your product, but for whom the timing simply isn't right. When that happens, you will want your salespeople to maintain appropriate contact with those customers until they are again at the point in the itch cycle at which they are ready to purchase. Ideally, your salespeople will do this in a way that positions your company to be the customer's clear, unquestioned choice when it is time to make a new purchase.

Sales force automation technology can assure that this happens effortlessly. Once a prospect is entered into an automated contact management system, the necessary follow-up can be scheduled automatically. For example, a prospect can receive a different follow-up letter every month, with each letter emphasizing an important point about your product. In addition, a phone call to the prospect can be scheduled every 60 or 90 days, allowing your salesperson to be in regular contact with the prospect. Finally, a reminder can be placed into the system for your salesperson to schedule an appointment with the prospect 30 days or so before the prospect is likely to buy again. All of this follow-up happens automatically; nothing gets overlooked or forgotten.

Not only does a sales automation system allow your salespeople to handle their prospects more efficiently, it also allows them to become more effective by handling a larger number of prospects. In the case of one company I studied, the average number of prospects that were maintained in the prospect pipeline before the introduction of a sales force automation system was 175. Twelve months after the system was introduced, that average had increased to over 500! This happened naturally because the system made it much easier for the salespeople to maintain the larger number of contacts. How much more effective do you think your sales staff would be if their average prospect pipeline could be increased almost threefold?

Eliminate Administrative Time Wasters

As we discussed earlier, most salespeople are forced to spend inordinate amounts of time on activities that are administrative in nature, a trend that is getting worse rather than better. Sales force automation technology offers sales managers a way to salvage this wasted time.

As an example, let's consider the traditional approach to reporting that is usually taken by the manager of a field-based sales force. In most companies, salespeople are required to submit two types of reports regularly: calendars and sales call reports. The calendar is a weekly or monthly listing of appointments that the salesperson has with clients or prospects; the sales call report details the results of those appointments after they take place. Both reports are primarily tools through which management can monitor the activity and performance of salespeople. (The sales call report ostensibly serves the secondary function of letting management know what is going on with customers. In practice, this is often not the case. One salesperson I know regularly includes in his sales call reports outlandish, fabricated tales of sex and intrigue at client sites. His sales manager has never given any indication of actually having read any of the reports.)

Calendar Reports

As a sales manager, it is, of course, necessary and reasonable that you have the information contained in these reports. But it is not uncommon that these reports take away as much as an hour per week from each salesperson's schedule. The amount of wasted time becomes somewhat ironic when you consider the fact that much of the information in these reports duplicates information that salespeople must keep for themselves! The calendar report, for example, contains precisely the same information that appears in the salesperson's own calendar or appointment book. (A few companies allow their salespeople to simply photocopy the relevant scheduling pages, but well over 90 percent of the companies that I have worked with require that the information be duplicated in a different format.)

A sales force automation system eliminates this redundancy and removes the need for separate reporting. First of all, the salesperson's calendar or appointment book is replaced with the scheduling portion of a sales force automation software package. Appointments are then scheduled, using the computer instead of pen and paper. There are two immediate advantages to doing this. First, having appointments electronically linked to the relevant contact and account information, including phone numbers, directions, etc., eliminates the risk of not having that information conveniently available when it is needed. Second, appointments that are recorded electronically are far easier to reschedule.

Once your salesperson has created his or her schedule, it can be easily transmitted to you on a weekly or even on a daily basis. The salesperson needs to do nothing more than record his or her own appointments (which, of course, he or she must do anyway), and the calendar report is derived automatically.

Sales Call Reports

Substantially the same thing happens with sales call reports. Sales force automation software allows a salesperson to make notes on the results of any sales call or telephone conversation. Like the salesperson's schedule, these notes are something that most salespeople would jot down for their own benefit, so no extra work is required. (An added benefit to this approach is the fact that, since these notes tend to be brief and to the point, they are more likely to get read by most sales managers than lengthy sales call reports. If the manager wants more detailed information on a particular event, he or she always has the option of asking for it.)

And, like the calendar, the sales call notes are part of the information package that the salesperson electronically forwards to management on a weekly or daily basis.

The automation of calendar and sales call reports alone can save most field-based salespeople over an hour per week. If we assume, for the sake of illustration, that salespeople spend approximately 20 hours per week actually selling (a generous assumption), then this extra hour of selling time could translate into an immediate 5 percent gain before any of the other benefits of sales force automation are realized! When the other efficiencies that we have examined are added in, it is clear that the streamlining of certain administrative tasks and the outright elimination of others can have an impact of several orders of magnitude on a salesperson's available selling time. If it is true that salespeople should be selling, then sales force automation is the means whereby they find the time to do so.

We did a survey with the help of Anderson consulting. It showed us that our salespeople are gaining about a day and a half per month of additional selling time. That is an extra selling month every year!

JOHN WILLIAMS
Storage Technology

Make Sales Calls More Effective

Not only can sales automation technology give your salespeople more time to sell, it can also help make the time that they spend selling more productive. It can do this in a variety of ways, depending on the particular needs of your organization. But there is a common denominator that can be found throughout many different and diverse implementations. That common denominator is the ability of computers to deliver information quickly and to present that information in a suitable and appropriate format.

Electronic Product Catalog

An increasingly common example is the electronic product catalog. This is an application of sales automation technology that is finding favor with companies whose salespeople used to lug around cumbersome, complicated product catalogs. This is particularly true in a field such as industrial sales, where a manufacturer's catalog can often include tens of thousands of parts, traditionally spread out over two or more extremely thick three-ring binders. Obviously, under those circumstances it can be challenging to have to locate a particular part in the catalog! Not only that, but most salespeople are awkward when they need to look something up in front of a customer. At best, it can interrupt the flow of a sales call; at worst, it can make the salesperson appear to be unprepared or unfamiliar with his or her products, even when that is not the case.

Another characteristic of the traditional catalog is that the information must be organized in one particular way, perhaps by function or by product category. Because a single method of organization is seldom sufficient, many catalogs are produced with a cross-reference index, increasing the utility of the catalog, but also increasing its bulk.

One of our best salespeople used to carry around a cardboard mockup of an instrument panel. He would literally cut out pictures of different options and paste them on the mockup to show a customer what a certain configuration would look like. Now, our salespeople can use the computer to create an illustration of a customer's instrument panel right on the spot. And that illustration can be attached to the customer's purchase order, so there are no questions about what a particular configuration was supposed to look like.

BRAD BARNES
McDonnell Douglas Helicopter

An electronic product catalog compresses the information found in several large loose-leaf binders and fits it all into a six-pound notebook computer, making the information physically less awkward to manipulate. More important, though, is the fact that an electronic catalog organizes the information in a way that is far more versatile than a traditional catalog. An item or a group of items in the catalog can be found by its product category, its function, its price, or by one or two key words in its description. This is because an electronic catalog is, at its heart, a database and, therefore, has the same type of searching capabilities that any database has.

Visual Support

As the graphic capabilities of computers increase, the possibilities for electronic catalogs are commensurately enhanced. Instead of merely accessing information, the electronic catalog becomes a presentation tool, as well. Real estate agents, for example, can now keep color photographs of houses stored on their computer. When they determine what a client's requirements are, they can search through their listings to select a group of houses that meet those requirements. They can then display color photos of the selected properties right on the computer screen.

One company I know has enhanced its catalog by including brief movies of its products in action! Once one of their salespeople finds a particular product in the catalog, he or she can then press a key that will cause the computer to display a 20-second movie of the product being used! In both of these instances, computer technology enhances the effectiveness of a sales call by adding visual impact and intelligence to what would otherwise be a simple product listing in a catalog.

Inventory Inquiry

A final example of how sales automation can increase the effectiveness of sales calls is in the area of inventory inquiry. Customers often would like to know about a product's availability before ordering. Sometimes this can be handled by a quick telephone call to the office. As the availability of sales support decreases, however, it is no longer as easy as it once was to find someone who can track this kind of information down while your salesperson waits on the phone in the customer's office. What happens, instead, is that the salesperson promises to find out about product availability upon returning to the office. While this is an understandable fallback, it is clear that the momentum of the sales call is often lost, and sometimes the order is lost along with it.

The proper sales automation system will allow the salesperson to check inventory status right from the client's office via modem. A skilled salesperson can then turn a simple availability inquiry into a closing opportunity. Once on-line with the warehouse, he or she can place the order, allocate the product, and receive confirmation of a shipping date all at the same time! Sales force automation can be a crucial factor in allowing a skilled salesperson to turn a question about the inventory status of a product into a completed sale!

> The price range for our products is between a half million dollars and 20 million dollars. So, they are big ticket items. Before our salespeople were automated, from the start to the finish of our typical sales cycle there would be approximately 50 customer contacts to get an order. Now after one year, we are down to 40 contacts to get an order. That is a tremendous productivity increase.
>
> JOHN WILLIAMS
> *Storage Technology*

Summary

Sales force automation can make salespeople more efficient and more effective. It creates more time for them to spend in front of customers by allowing them to fulfill the administrative requirements of their jobs more quickly (and more accurately, as well). It also helps them to be more effective when they are in front of customers.

4

Truly Superior Customer Service Is Automated

American business has gone through tremendous upheaval during the past decade. While the process was sometimes difficult, the hard-won lessons were valuable and have provided the foundation for increased competitiveness and productivity. Of all the lessons that were learned, none was quite as fundamental or profound as the rediscovery of the critical importance of customer satisfaction.

Customer Satisfaction— The Only Unassailable Competitive Advantage

Customers are the lifeblood of any business. And in the business environment of the 1990s and beyond, it is increasingly true that the only sustainable competitive advantage is customer satisfaction. At one time a company could distinguish itself in the marketplace through its products or through its pricing. These advantages alone can no longer provide long-term protection.

Even industries that are based on technologically sophisticated products have found that their products can be quickly duplicated or imitated by competitors. And industry after industry has found that it is impossible to establish a price point that is so low that a competitor will not attempt to get lower, even if it is unprofitable to do so.

It is clear that only satisfied customers can provide a company with long-term security in the hypercompetitive marketplace of the twenty-first century. Customer satisfaction is the only long-term, sustainable competitive advantage.

This book is not an appropriate place for me to get on my soapbox about the importance of taking care of customers, so I will refrain from doing so. I will assume that your company has an abiding commitment to customer satisfaction. (If it does not, then it is unlikely that even the power of sales force automation technology will do much good in the long run.)

The real issue, then, is identifying the most effective means of making certain that your customers are satisfied. The first point to be made here is that, for many companies, the sales force provides all or most of the contact that customers have with the company. Often, salespeople are the only people who will speak regularly with your customers. And, more important, it is the salesperson who will usually get the call from a customer who has a question or a problem. This being the case, it will be no surprise to you, I am sure, to learn that many companies are finding sales force automation technology to be an extremely powerful tool that is helping them to achieve that objective.

We can see why this is true by first defining some of the more significant component parts of customer satisfaction, then examining the role that sales force automation can play in supporting each of those components. A list like this is not intended to be a comprehensive definition of customer satisfaction, but any discussion of the subject will certainly include the following ingredients. Customers want:

- Timely and accurate information about their orders
- Prompt and dependable answers to questions
- Follow through on commitments within the promised time frame
- Regular contact

Your company's ability to perform in all of these areas can be enhanced with the introduction of a sales automation system.

Expectations and Perceptions

Any discussion of customer satisfaction should also recognize this important truth: Customer satisfaction is influenced more by expectations and perceptions than it is by any objective reality. Customers will generally be more satisfied with a company that meets their expectations than they will with a company that delivers better performance—when measured by an objective standard—but does not meet the customer's level of expectation. Sales managers who instruct their salespeople to "undercommit and overdeliver" are well aware of this principle. A customer who expects an order to arrive in ten days will be extremely pleased if it arrives in five. If a second customer expected the order to get there in three days, though, four days would be unsatisfactory even though it is a day earlier than the first customer's order. A salesperson could always provide a delivery date with a hedge, but he or she would then have to weigh the risk of not getting the order at all. There is a precarious balance that needs to be achieved.

Similarly, customers will tend to be dissatisfied with a company that they perceive to be deficient in performance, whether that company is actually deficient or not. And that perception can often be caused by factors that have no logical relationship to the immediate situation. Several years ago, the chief executive of a major airline made the observation, "If we have dirty tray tables, our customers will assume that we do a poor job at engine maintenance as well." He understood the dynamics of how customers' perceptions operate.

Access to Information

The ability of your salespeople to quickly obtain accurate information is critical to customer satisfaction. Your customers want information about their orders, and they want answers to their questions. Sales automation can provide both.

In Chapter 1, we discussed the productivity impact that an electronic catalog can have on your sales efforts. This ability to put large amounts of information about your products and services in the hands of your salespeople can yield important benefits in the demesne of customer satisfaction as well. If a customer has a question about a particular item that your company offers, your salesperson will have instant access to that product's price and specifications.

> Salespeople cannot be knowledgeable or act in a consultative role without information. And they have to be able to get at that information easily. There is a lot of data out there, but it only becomes usable information if people can access it.
>
> KEVIN FLYNN
> *Apple Computer*

Many companies have extended this concept further by providing their salespeople with specifications and pricing information on competitive products. This enables salespeople to function in a consultative role, providing their customers with the information they need to make an informed decision. Sales automation also provides a convenient way for your company to make certain that your salespeople have information that is current and accurate and that the information is presented in a uniform manner across your sales staff.

In addition to product information, customers often want to know about things like product availability and sales order status. An automation system that accesses this type of information yields perceptible customer satisfaction benefits as well as the productivity advantages discussed in Chapter 3.

By using a dial-in connection to access information that is stored on a computer at the office, your salespeople can immediately respond to customer inquiries with data that is up to the minute and accurate. This allows them to be more responsive to your customers' needs. This increased ability to be of service to customers will allow your salespeople to forge relationships that are collaborative and cooperative rather than strained or confrontational.

> We decided that we wanted our salespeople to be real partners with our customers. In order to do that, they needed to have all the necessary business facts at their fingertips, all of the latest sales information, sales order status, back order status, cancellations, everything.
>
> DAVID JOY
> *Stanley Tools*

Used in this way, sales automation enhances customer satisfaction by enabling your salespeople to bring demonstrable value to the relationship with the customer.

Eliminating the "Cracks"

Customer satisfaction is the end result of customer service. And customer service, at its most basic, consists of doing the things that our customers expect of us (and, perhaps a little more), particularly those things about which we have made commitments. If we say that we are going to deliver a product on a certain date, we should do it. If we say that we will call back next week, then that is when we should call. In theory, nothing should be simpler.

In reality, though, the business world is complex and fast-paced. I doubt that there is a sales manager anywhere who has not had the experience of listening to a salesperson explain how something just "fell through the cracks." It might be that a sale was lost because a customer did not receive a promised call back because your salesperson simply forgot. Or it might be that a lead from a trade show was never called at all because your salesperson lost the slip of paper you gave him or her with the phone number.

It is tempting to adopt a hard-line stance in these situations, treating them as the business world's equivalent of "The dog ate my homework." While I don't suggest that you cavalierly excuse these kinds of oversights, I want to point out that your interests as a sales manager are better served by identifying and addressing the underlying causes and by assuming responsibility for getting them fixed.

> Sales force automation has allowed us to achieve a level of customer satisfaction that really distinguishes us from our competition.
>
> WILLIAM FRIEL
> *Goodyear Tire and Rubber*

A good place to start is to take responsibility for the kinds of tools that your salespeople use to attend to the details of their job. Regardless of what your salespeople are using now, a sales force automation system will prove to be superior in every way.

Names and addresses, directions, product preferences, and any other pertinent facts about a customer need be entered into the system only once. The information is then easily available and accessible to anyone who might need it. Assuming the system is well designed and properly maintained, the information cannot get lost.

Along these lines, consider the "Mackay 66" from Harvey Mackay's classic book, "Swim With the Sharks Without Getting Eaten Alive." The "Mackay 66" is a set of questions about a customer or prospect, the answers to which Mackay believes a successful salesperson must uncover over a period of time in order to be truly effective. The "Mackay 66" is controversial and I have heard it discussed often by sales managers. A frequent comment is that acquiring the kind of detailed information about a customer that Mackay suggests made sense in theory, but would be extremely difficult to accomplish in practice.

With a sales automation system, even information in the degree of detail that Mackay proposes can be tracked with comparative ease. (Harvey Mackay, in conjunction with software developer CogniTech, has just come out with *Sharkware*, a contact manager that also automates the tracking of the "Mackay 66.")

Mackay points out that the more a salesperson knows about a client, the more effective that salesperson is likely to be. I would add that the more a salesperson knows about a prospect or customer, the more likely it is that that salesperson will be able to address that person's individual needs. And, when that happens regularly, customer satisfaction is the inevitable result.

> An intelligently designed sales force automation system gives a company the ability to do much more customized fitting of products to potential customers' needs.
>
> WARREN MACFARLAND
> *Harvard Business School*

The ability to keep track of follow-up items is particularly important in the pursuit of customer satisfaction. Any commitment that is made to a customer, no matter how small or seemingly insignificant, must be kept. If a customer is expecting a phone call on Monday, then Tuesday is not good enough. If a salesperson tells a customer or prospect that they will get a call back with the answer to a question, then that is exactly what must happen. The lesson behind the story about airline tray tables and engine maintenance is appropriate here. Our customers will judge us on our ability to follow through on small commitments. If we do not perform flawlessly on small tasks, then we will not get the opportunity to try for the large ones. Once a follow-up item is entered into the computer, it cannot be lost, overlooked, or forgotten by a salesperson until it is completed. Moreover, unlike a salesperson's manual calendar or appointment book, a sales force automation system makes these follow-up items available for management review, providing an additional backstop to prevent an important item from being neglected.

The unique advantage of a sales automation system, though, is not that it can handle a great deal of information but that it can handle that information efficiently for an extremely large number of contacts. Of course, it is not particularly difficult to maintain a large number of contacts as long as you don't have to do anything with them! It is easy to accumulate a large contact file over a period of time, if that is all that you are trying to do. What makes dealing with a great many contacts challenging and difficult is that each contact has a right to expect to be treated as though he or she is the only prospect or customer in the world. Sales force automation makes this kind of individualized attention possible.

Tactics

In some sales situations, it is advisable to have a salesperson follow a predetermined sequence of events. For example, you might determine that a telephone inquiry might be handled in this way:

1. Send catalog (same day as initial phone call)
2. Telephone to schedule appointment (three days after catalog is sent)
3. Appointment
4. Thank-you letter (day after appointment)
5. Follow-up visit and close (four days after appointment)

In this example, sending the catalog and making the phone call to schedule the appointment are triggered by the customer's telephone inquiry. The thank-you letter and the follow-up visit are triggered by the completion of the initial appointment. If you have determined that this is the sequence of events that you want your salespeople to follow for every prospect, then it is important that the follow-up items are not left to chance. They need to happen automatically every time.

With a sales force automation system, the sending of the catalog and the phone call to schedule the follow-up appointment would be automatically scheduled by the system. The possibility is eliminated that these follow-up steps in the sales process will be forgotten or overlooked. In addition, since these steps are programmed into the system, you are able to achieve a high degree of uniformity throughout your sales force in the area of follow-up after an inquiry. Every potential customer can experience the same quality of service at every step in the sales process.

This kind of follow-up can be extended beyond the sales process, as well. It is often in the area of after-the-sale follow-up that the biggest opportunities to enhance customer satisfaction exist. For example, if you sell a product that has a limited manufacturer's warranty, your sales force automation system can be designed to notify the salesperson a couple of weeks before the warranty expires so that the customer can be offered the opportunity to purchase extended coverage. What kind of customer satisfaction do you think results when a customer's equipment breaks a week after the warranty expires? It might not be your fault that such an unfortunate event occurred, but when it does, experience demonstrates that you will be the recipient of your customer's anger and frustration. If, on the other hand, your sales automation system reminded your salesperson to call the customer about the impending loss of warranty coverage (particularly if the system records when and by whom such a call was made), then your customer winds up with little reason to be dissatisfied with your service. (Moreover, if your salesperson was skilled and tenacious enough to actually get the sale on the extended coverage, then you will wind up with a customer who is absolutely delighted.)

Another example of after-the-sale follow-up would be to have the system automatically schedule a phone call by your salesperson to the customer at the six-month anniversary of any major purchase. The purpose of the call would be to verify that the customer is pleased with the product or service. This kind of follow-up will:

- Give you a terrific opportunity to make certain that there are no unknown, unresolved problems or issues that would benefit from your company's attention
- Give your salesperson an opportunity to make additional, add-on sales
- Create a tremendous amount of satisfaction among your customers because none of your competitors takes the time and trouble to do this

The key to successful customer service, again, is the fact that the sales system makes it happen automatically. Nothing gets overlooked. Nothing is forgotten. Nothing falls through the cracks.

Emerson once said, "A foolish consistency is the hobgoblin of small minds." That may be true, but it is also true that an unfailing consistency in the areas of performance and follow through is the foundation for superior customer satisfaction.

Accurate Communications

Your company, like most other companies, is doubtlessly composed of a number of departments. And, if you are like other companies, then it is probably true that communications among these various departments is not always perfect. Your customer can probably understand this most of the time, but the unfortunate truth is that customers who have a problem are not always at their most rational. For those customers, it is simply not acceptable to have the fingers of your employees pointing in various directions when they are trying to get some answers.

As we have seen, a sales force automation system will often act primarily as a communications system. In this capacity, it can be the foundation of a customer information system that allows everyone in your company, not just the sales department, to have access to the information that they need to take care of your customers.

Truly great customer service—and therefore customer satisfaction—comes from creating a perception that everything is perfect. That perception cannot be sustained if a salesperson has to call in to the office to double-check on the status of an order. Similarly, the perception fails if the people in billing don't know that a customer has renewed a maintenance agreement and, as a result, send out a bill for service that shouldn't be sent. Properly implemented, sales force automation technology allows everyone involved with your customer to be updated almost on a real-time basis so there is no excuse for people not having current information about a customer's situation.

GIL CARGILL
IDK Group

A sales force automation system can help your salespeople keep track of such pieces of information as:

- Conversations that various employees have with customers on important or sensitive issues
- The status of orders, credits, accounts
- What pieces of equipment a customer has on site

Ultimately, your customers want answers to questions and solutions to problems. A sales force automation system can provide the framework that allows your company, its salespeople, and its other employees to deliver both.

Summary

Customer satisfaction is the most significant factor in customer retention. The willingness to do what is necessary to enhance customer satisfaction is a key component of the strategic plans of many companies in the 1990s. Sales force automation technology can be an indispensable tool in achieving the responsiveness, thoroughness, and quality of service that leads to customer satisfaction.

5
The Strategic Advantage of Speed

When Tom Peters devotes an entire television show to making a single point, there is probably something going on that is noteworthy enough to deserve our attention. In 1992, Peters did just that. His PBS show detailed the significance of speed as a competitive advantage. Although Tom Peters tends to focus on the manufacturing process rather than the sales process, his point is as valid for sales managers as it is for factory managers. As product cycles shorten and the pace of competition accelerates, those companies which are able to execute more quickly will have a demonstrable advantage in an extremely competitive marketplace.

> If you are in a competitive situation, your competitor is right behind you as soon as you leave your customer's office. If you have a potential customer who wants something right away, you need to be able to respond immediately. Our competitor might have to tell the customer that it is going to be a week before they get a proposal. We want to have the deal closed by the time our competition is ready to respond.
>
> RON MENZEL
> *Holmes Protection*

That the pace of competition is accelerating is undeniable. A classic example is one that I mentioned in the Introduction. In the airline industry, price wars used to evolve over a period of weeks. An airline would lower its price and competitors would respond after gauging the market's reaction over a period of time. Today's hypercompetitive environment does not allow for such leisurely reflection. Price wars now erupt within hours, at levels of intensity that are great enough to generate newspaper headlines the next day. If a player in the market is unable to respond immediately to revolutionary changes in fare structures, then the market simply leaves that player behind. Catch-up is a difficult and decidedly unrewarding game to play.

Other competitive realities are also placing a premium on speed. Businesses are loath to carry inventory in their warehouses or on their balance sheets. Instead, they are adopting an inventory policy that calls for "just in time" delivery of goods. As a result, suppliers are being forced to be more responsive to the needs of their customers and to develop systems that address those needs.

Corporate downsizing has also contributed to the importance of speed. Purchasing departments, understaffed compared to just a few years ago, are being forced to operate with less and less lead time. This trend also reinforces the need for speed and responsiveness on the part of suppliers.

Shortening Sales and Delivery Cycles

As these trends make themselves felt throughout the business community, sales managers are increasingly desirous of tools that will allow them to respond more quickly to the needs of their customers. Sales force automation is a powerful tool that helps sales managers do exactly that.

We have already seen in Chapter 3 how the sales process itself can be shortened by the use of automated, intelligent proposal and configuration systems, so we will not spend a great deal of time replowing that particular field. It is sufficient to point out that the enhanced responsiveness that is made possible when

> Our sales proposals used to take us an average of 10 working days to get done. They had to be approved by the district manager so that we were certain that the content was right from a legal standpoint. Then, the financial services manager would make sure the pricing was right. A systems engineer or a customer service engineer had to make sure that the system configuration was technically correct. And, of course, the whole thing had to be put into a professional-looking format. By the time the entire process was completed, it took about 10 days. We have eliminated a great deal of that process because of the intelligence built into the system. One of our salespeople can now get a proposal done within a half hour. That is a huge difference.
>
> JOHN WILLIAMS
> *Storage Technology*

those systems are automated can be a critical point of differentiation in a competitive situation. My research for this book uncovered numerous instances where a salesperson using an automated proposal system was able to preempt the competition altogether, securing an order before a competitor was even able to make a proposal. One of the reasons for this is that the speed with which the salesperson is able to respond to the customer *before* the order increases the customer's confidence that the salesperson and his or her company will be able to respond quickly *after* the order as well.

For the purposes of this discussion, though, I would like to concentrate on the ways in which sales force automation speeds up the sales cycle after a customer's order is placed. Sales cycles can, of course, vary dramatically from company to company and from one product to another. Moreover, the saving of several days in a sales cycle that otherwise would have taken a week is clearly much more dramatic than a similar saving in a cycle of a month. But, regardless of the length of the baseline sales cycle, the fact remains that, once an order is placed, customers almost always prefer to receive their purchases sooner rather than later.

Electronic Transmission of Sales Orders

The most straightforward way in which sales automation can shorten the sales cycle is by using an automated system to electronically transmit a sales order instantly from the notebook computer of the salesperson in the field directly to the company's order-processing department.

The least elegant variation on this theme would call for the salesperson to send either an electronic fax file or a text file containing the sales order information. In the former case, it would be necessary for the order to be rekeyed into the company's main system once it reached headquarters; in the latter case, such rekeying might be necessary, but it is possible that this redundant effort could be avoided, depending on some specific characteristics of the main system software. While neither of these methods is necessarily ideal, either one would save the several days that it would otherwise take to have the orders submitted by mail.

Another approach would allow the salesperson to access the company's main computer and enter his or her orders directly into the main system. This type of connection is relatively easy to accomplish and has the advantage of speed. On the other hand, this is not always the most convenient approach from the salesperson's standpoint.

The most sophisticated, and most efficient, approach would allow a salesperson to create a sales order on his or her notebook computer, and then transmit the completed sales order over telephone lines in a format that could be read directly by the company's main computer system. This approach allows a salesperson to complete an order at his or her convenience. Given the realities of working in the field, this probably means completing the order in a piecemeal fashion using bits of time between appointments.

> When we first gave our salespeople hand-held computer systems, we projected that we would be able to cut turnaround time in the order processing cycle—from the time that the order was taken and until the time that it was entered into our main computer—from approximately 10 days on average to 2 working days. And that is exactly what we did.
>
> DAVID JOY
> *Stanley Tools*

The net result of any one of these approaches is that a sales order reaches the order-processing department several days faster than it would without the availability of automation technology. Transmitting the order so that it does not have to be rekeyed eliminates an additional day or two from the sales order cycle.

Automated Credit Checks

As we search through the sales order cycle for bottlenecks, our attention next comes to rest on the credit approval process. It is not uncommon for a salesperson to encounter some kind of credit problem that prevents his or her customer from receiving an order in a timely fashion. While this kind of situation cannot be avoided, it is usually not until several days after the order is placed that the salesperson finds out that there is a problem. When this happens, the salesperson has lost those several days from the sales order cycle and is then back at square one, needing to address the customer's problem before the order gets processed. More often than most companies would care to admit, the salesperson does not find out that there is a problem until the customer calls up looking for the order! Most salespeople have found themselves in this situation. They can describe the uncomfortable feeling of being placed in the middle of a confrontation, with the customer wanting his or her order on one side and the company wanting its money on the other. This is, of course, not an unsolvable situation. But it is much more likely that a problem will yield a satisfactory solution when it is addressed sooner rather than later.

> You stand a much greater chance of making the sale if you can provide your customer with the information that he or she needs right there and then—either because it is already on your machine or because you can access it over a phone line
>
> KEVIN FLYNN
> *Apple Computer*

Sales automation can provide the salesperson with the capability of ascertaining a customer's credit status through an on-line inquiry. This would allow a salesperson to deal with a problematic credit situation before it delayed the delivery of a customer's order. The result is not only that the sales order cycle is shortened, but also that customer satisfaction is enhanced simultaneously.

How Speed Kills (the Competition)

The principle to keep in mind in the pursuit of speed is that your ability to respond to your customers quickly is a strategic weapon that can distinguish you from your competitors.

Your ability to shorten the sales order cycles means that you are delivering value to your customers by increasing the convenience of doing business with your company. It also means that your customer can decrease the amount of inventory that he or she carries, since you have the ability to replenish more quickly any inventory that is sold or used.

> We found that the systems allowed us to react a lot faster to our customer because we could deliver the product to them a lot faster. At first, we were concerned that we would wind up with more orders at a lower dollar amount per order. Well, the reality was that orders started to grow because our customers started to carry more Stanley products. This was because they could get them more efficiently when they wanted them. They would have an order at their doorstep within three to four working days instead of ten to twenty working days.
>
> DAVID JOY
> *Stanley Tools*

Although helping your customer manage inventory is important, it is not the only area of your customers' balance sheet that you can positively impact through the use of sales force automation technology. A well-designed system will also allow you to process customer credits more rapidly. This means that less of your customers' money will be tied up in administrative limbo. Clearly, being able to make meaningful improvements in this area can translate into a significant competitive advantage.

> We constantly hear from competitive dealers that it takes them forever to get credits back from their suppliers. Our system speeds that process up tremendously. So what we are really doing is enhancing our level of service to our customers.
>
> WILLIAM FRIEL
> *Goodyear Tire and Rubber*

These are the "value added" areas that, in the future, will serve to differentiate your company from its competitors. And this value can be delivered only by those companies which find ways to respond quickly to customers needs and to move rapidly in the marketplace. These improvements can be made only by those companies which learn how to make effective use of sales force automation technology.

Summary

Speed is an increasingly important ingredient in a successful assault on the competition. The ability to respond quickly to customer inquiries and the ability to deliver products and services more quickly than competitors are key factors in maintaining a competitive posture in the marketplace of the 1990s.

Sales force automation technology allows companies to respond more quickly to the challenges of the marketplace. It is the fastest way to deliver information to where it is needed.

6
Enhanced Professionalism

I believe that it is relatively easy to cost justify a sales force automation system. There are so many examples in this book of ways to increase sales productivity and to simultaneously lower the costs associated with selling that return-on-investment analysis seems self-evident. When I began to write this book, I made the assumption that every sales manager who had undertaken the expense associated with automating his or her sales force had done so with some variation of a cost-justification scenario in mind. I was wrong.

What we are selling is state-of-the-art security services. But most of our customers will never actually see any of our equipment until it is installed. They only see the sales person who sells the system. So it is extremely important that we present a professional image, an image that supports the fact that we are offering state-of-the-art technology. The salesperson is the only part of our company that the customer sees. Our sales force automation system says to our customers that we have invested in technology right down to the salesperson.

RON MENZEL
Holmes Protection

Among the dozens of companies I interviewed that had implemented some form of sales force automation system, I was surprised to find that at least one-third had done so with no cost-justification objectives or return-on-investment analysis whatsoever. And among the companies that had looked at these factors, at least half had done so as an afterthought, fully intending to automate regardless of how the numbers looked.

The very fact that we have made the investment to put computers in the hands of our salespeople, the fact that our salespeople have instant access to this kind of information, speaks volumes about the type of company we are. How do you put a value on that?

DAVID JOY
Stanley Tools

Tending to approach these kinds of issues conservatively, I was intrigued by this attitude and, of course, asked each of the managers involved about the factors that were driving their decisions. In every case, the answer was the same. Manager after manager told me that he or she believed that sales force automation would enhance the professionalism of their sales force. These managers further believed that the perception by their customers of an enhanced professionalism among their salespeople by itself would be enough to justify an investment in a sales automation system.

As enthusiastic as I am about the benefits of sales force automation, I think that companies ought to be using more substantial criteria in making this decision. Having said that, however, it is also true that sales force automation technology can tremendously enhance the professionalism and persuasiveness of salespeople.

Professionalism Enhances Persuasiveness

The traditional perception of the sales process centers on the sales presentation. Although this is a very limited perception of the sales process, it is certainly true that presentation skills represent an important part of the complete package of skills that we look for in sales professionals. Sales presentations, in order to be effective, must be:

- Complete
- Concise
- Informative
- Authoritative
- Professional and polished

Computer technology can enhance all of these qualities in a sales presentation.

More Professional Presentations

Most of the companies studied for this book had created the presentations used by their salespeople with software that is specially designed for this purpose. (*Persuasion* by Aldus Corporation is an example of this category of software.) Presentations are created by entering an outline of the material that is to be covered in the final presentation. This outline is then automatically converted by the software into a presentation format that can be inexpensively transferred onto 35mm slides or overhead transparencies.

Alternatively, it is becoming increasingly common to use the computer itself for the presentations. For a one-on-one presentation, or for a small group, a presentation can be given right off the screen of a notebook computer. For larger groups, a color LCD panel can be attached to the computer. The LCD screen can then be placed on an overhead projector, allowing an entire roomful of people to see a presentation directly from the computer.

In either case, it should first be noted that these computer-generated presentations are relatively inexpensive. Even in those situations where 35mm or overheads must be created, the cost of a typical presentation generated using presentation software is approximately one-fourth to one-fifth of what a similar presentation would have cost five years ago. When presentations are given using an LCD screen or directly from a computer screen, the total cost is, of course, even less.

Presentations Can Be Customized

The presentations that are given directly from the computer, however, have at least one important advantage. Because of the ease with which they are created, these computer-generated presentations are easy to modify. And while most companies do not require salespeople to have the artistic skills to create a presentation from scratch, computer technology allows presentations to be easily customized by the salesperson for specific clients. With this approach, salespeople start out with a standard presentation, or "template," created by the company. It is then modified so that the resulting presentation is specific and individualized to the customer or prospect.

> The fact of the matter is that customers were extremely impressed with what we were doing. It enhanced the image of our company and made it easier for customers to make that decision to buy from us.
>
> JOHN WILLIAMS
> *Storage Technology*

The results can be extremely powerful. Customers, instead of having to sit through generic presentations, are able to see facts and figures that are specific to them. As a result, they find the customized presentations more engaging, more involving, and more persuasive.

This use of computer technology for sales presentations creates a situation that combines the best elements of predesigned presentations with the immediacy and individuality of presentations that are created by salespeople. Sales presentations that are "canned" have the advantages of being thorough, professional-looking, and accurate. Management often gravitates toward this approach because these presentations cover all of the important points, and do so in a way that is known to avoid unintentional misrepresentation. Moreover, the cost of creating an entirely new presentation for each client is prohibitive, both in terms of time and money.

Individualized presentations, on the other hand, have the advantage of being focused and specific. Customers are much more likely to become involved with a presentation that appears to be designed just for them.

Computer-based presentation technology is powerful and flexible enough to address both sets of concerns. Since the framework of a computer-based presentation is designed by the company, it is professional-looking and accurate and it covers all of the points that management wants to make about its products or services. But because of the ease with which presentation software allows for modification, it can be personalized for each customer or prospect by the salesperson.

Multimedia

The advantages of computer-based presentations extend far beyond their flexibility. The power of today's notebook computers allows companies to inexpensively create presentations that are unlike anything that has been feasible in the past. Computer-based presentations can now include much more than the standard visual and graphic elements. In fact, those standard elements have become merely the foundation on which presentations are built. On that foundation, salespeople can now incorporate video and audio elements that can create powerful effects.

This incorporation of video and audio elements into traditional presentation technology has created a new category of computer technology known as multimedia. And, as has been the case with so many other aspects of computer technology, it is only recently that technological advances have allowed the power of multimedia to be made portable and, therefore, suitable for use by salespeople based in the field.

Affordable and Portable Presentations

From a hardware standpoint, multimedia requires that a computer have adequate capabilities in three areas:

1. *Sound capability.* The hardware should be able to play sound

through an internal speaker or to route stereo sound through a pair of external speakers connected to the computer.

2. *Appropriate video capability.*   Most of the computers sold today have video capabilities that can accommodate multimedia.

3. *Adequate storage.*   Because audio and video require large amounts of storage, extensive multimedia usually requires a CD ROM drive and a storage device that plays disks that are substantially identical to the CDs that you buy in a music store.

Each of these capabilities can easily be added to existing notebook computers.

The graphics capabilities of a Macintosh computer can make a tremendous difference in what a typical sales presentation looks like. A salesperson might include a *QuickTime* movie of the company's chief scientist describing the technical merits of a new product, as an example. If you are selling high-ticket items, you cannot wheel a giant machine into a customer's office for a demonstration. But you can bring a movie or a graphic that shows how your product could fit into your customer's existing environment. Or, if you are selling pharmaceuticals, you could include a computer-generated, animated presentation of how a particular drug might interact with different kinds of cell structures. This capability can really enhance and change the nature of sales presentations.

KEVIN FLYNN
Apple Computer

Multimedia technology incorporated into sales presentations significantly enhances the salesperson's ability to communicate. Computer-based audio and video give him or her the capability of illustrating products or concepts that have previously been difficult to present using a single visual medium of slides or overheads. And, the fact that these presentations are computer-based creates some important advantages over what can be done with a standard, videotaped presentation.

First, as we have noted, computer-based presentations are

much more portable than presentations using other media. It is not necessary to have access to a video machine; it is only necessary for the salesperson to carry a six-pound notebook computer (which, of course, the salesperson is also using for contact management, calendars, electronic mail, and a variety of the other tasks that we have discussed), and possibly an LCD screen if the presentation is to be made for several people.

Interactive Presentations

The most compelling advantage of computer-based multimedia presentations is that they can be made to be interactive, a feat that cannot easily be accomplished with traditional video. An interactive presentation is one that can be responsive to a customer's questions or concerns. If a customer is interested in service policies, the salesperson can immediately access that topic. If a customer is not interested in competitive comparisons, that section of the presentation can be skipped. A computer-based multimedia presentation is different from a traditional presentation in much the same way that a CD is different from a cassette tape. A CD can jump directly from one song to another, it can be programmed to rearrange the order in which songs are played, and it can bypass certain songs altogether. A cassette, on the other hand, must start at the beginning of one side and work its way through to the end. Of course, you can fast forward a cassette or flip it over, but you still do not have the instant, elegant access to the entire album that you have with a CD. Similarly, a computer-based presentation can be rearranged on the spot to reflect a customer's needs. It can be designed in a way that will allow a customer or salesperson to pick and choose topics and to explore them in whatever level of detail is desired.

The flexibility and power of computer-based presentations assure that they will forever change the standard against which sales presentations will be judged.

Which brings us full circle to the point that was made to me by so many of the companies with whom I spoke. Sales force automation enhances the professionalism of the sales force and the way in which the sales force is perceived by customers.

> At this stage of the game, sales force automation is a means of setting yourself apart from your competition. But pretty soon, it will be a matter of staying on par with the competition. If you are ahead of the game now, that's good. But you should know that if you haven't yet gotten started down this path, you will soon be behind the game.
>
>
>
> KEVIN FLYNN
> *Apple Computer*
>
>

Summary

In addition to the more quantifiable benefits of sales force automation, many companies are adopting sales force automation technology as a means of enhancing the professionalism of their salespeople. The use of sophisticated, computer-based presentations is one of the ways in which computers can contribute to the perception of professionalism.

PART 3

Giving Management a Winning Edge

7

Controlling Damage When a Top Performer Leaves

I will call him John. He used to own one of the largest computer reseller organizations on the East Coast. I was visiting with him at his office on a consulting project one afternoon and we started to discuss a problem that he was having with Dan, one of his top salespeople. Dan was threatening to go to work for one of John's competitors, and John was on the verge of panic.

"Here is the compensation plan that I am going to offer him." He pushed some papers across the desk. As I looked them over, I could not believe what I was reading.

"John, under this plan, not only will Dan make far more money on each sale than you do, but after your costs are factored in, it is difficult for me to see where you can make any money on his sales at all!"

"I know," John replied. "But what can I do? If he leaves, he takes all of his business with him. I don't know anything about his accounts or what is going on with them. He's got me painted into a corner."

I could follow this conversation through for you to its dismal conclusion, but I will spare you the sordid details. Since John really did know very little about Dan's customers, he was, indeed, painted into a corner. He offered Dan the outrageous compensation package that he showed me that afternoon. (Dan gobbled up the package and made an enormous amount of money at John's expense over the next year. He finally left anyway to go to work for John's competitor. When he did, he took most of his customers with him.)

The problem, from John's standpoint, is obvious. Those customers really were John's customers, not Dan's. It is true that Dan found them and cultivated them, but he did so as John's employee. John should have been able to hold his ground in any compensation discussions. If Dan's position became unreasonable, John should have been able to stand his ground and let Dan walk. John might have fought for the customers, but he would have gone into the battle with very little ammunition because John barely knew who his customers were. The little information that he had consisted of what he could glean from invoices. He did not know who the decision makers were, where each account was in the sales cycle, or how their management information systems (MIS) acquisition procedures worked.

Ensuring Continuity for Your Customers

Sales force automation has no magical properties that will prevent you from ever losing a top salesperson. Over a period of time, it is a certainty that you will, for a variety of reasons, lose some of your very best salespeople. Some will leave to go to work for a competitor, some will move out of town upon the relocation of a spouse, one or two might die, and—who knows—one might win the lottery and retire to live the life of luxury in Buenos Aires! For the purpose of this discussion, it does not matter why they leave. What matters is that you, as a sales manager, will be responsible for picking up the pieces when they do.

Picking up the pieces means that any personnel changes that occur should be virtually imperceptible to your customers. Your customer should experience no perceived discontinuity or disruption of service.

The customer service department at American Express is one of the finest examples that I have ever encountered of this principle in action. If you are an American Express cardholder and have a question or a problem, it does not matter when you call or who you talk to. The benefit of this system is apparent on those occasions when there is a problem whose resolution might take place over a period of several days. In similar situations with other companies, I will usually go to great lengths to make sure that I speak to the same person each time I call. In that way, I am spared the ordeal of having to explain my situation anew to every person with whom I come in contact.

With American Express, on the other hand, I have no such concern. Every question and conversation is permanently noted in the computer. All of the pertinent information is available on the computer to every customer service representative. It is possible to talk to three or four different representatives about the same issue and never have to repeat yourself. As a customer, this system never fails to impress me.

The customer service benefits of this type of system are obvious, as we have already seen in Chapter 4. Right now, though, we are focusing on the implications that this type of system has for you as a sales manager. In all likelihood, your account management structure is very different from the American Express model. If your account management structure is like most, each customer has one salesperson who is responsible for that customer's business.

In this model, it is not necessary for every salesperson to have access to information about every account. Until, of course, one of your salespeople leaves the company. When that happens, your attention immediately shifts to your customers. Your ability to take care of your customers is determined by how quickly you deliver the right information about them into the hands of the appropriate people in your company on a timely basis. The objective is continuity. Your customers ought to feel as though their interests have not been neglected when their salesperson leaves your company.

When salespeople leave, or when territories change hands, it is important to pay particular attention to:

- Orders that are in process
- Upcoming scheduled appointments and/or events
- Outstanding commitments

Traditionally, this information is conveyed, when possible, through the time-honored ritual of conveying notes and files to management or, occasionally, handing them over directly to the new salesperson responsible for the forsaken territory. (Of course, there are times when even this minimally effective effort does not occur. When a salesperson is fired, his or her notes and files often become a matter of contention. And, on those occasions when a salesperson leaves as a result of a tragedy, the conveyance of notes and files is sometimes not possible.) In theory, handing over notes and files ought to do the job. In practice, though, the results are often less than satisfying.

> We have had an extremely stable sales staff, but I know that turnover is a major concern for many sales managers. With a sales automation system like this in place, my job becomes much easier in terms of making certain that our customers are serviced properly.
>
> JAMES WEGLARZ
> *SmithKline Diagnostics*

For one thing, as we noted in Chapter 3, salespeople tend to not perform their administrative responsibilities with the thoroughness and attention to detail that we might want. As a result, the notes and files that exist are incomplete, indecipherable, and disorderly. The new salesperson gets what is usually a mess of paperwork, in no discernible order, and needs days or weeks to sort it all out, if it gets reviewed and sorted at all. If the goal of this process is to convey information that is usable, rather than merely a collection of papers and files, then the process is seldom successful. As a result, the new salesperson in the territory usually spends days or weeks recompiling the same information that already exists in the files. If this happens too often, customers eventually grow tired of explaining to new salespeople how they want their orders processed, and so they look elsewhere.

An automated sales system changes the nature of this process in several important ways. The first is that the structure of the system defines the nature of the record keeping. Therefore, every salesperson is tracking the same information in more or less the same way. The result of this consistency is that the records of any salesperson are immediately understandable by any other salesperson. Relevant or timely information is quickly apparent. The new salesperson in an account or territory can hit the ground running with a great deal of the necessary information at his or her fingertips.

Now we have information stored in our system on individual contacts at a customer site. Now, on those occasions when we do have a change in our personnel in the field, we have information available about our customers that we never had before. That is a real help for us, without a doubt.

WILLIAM FRIEL
Goodyear Tire and Rubber

More important, though, is the fact that the pertinent customer information is under your control, not under the control of your departing salesperson. There are a variety of reasons why a salesperson might leave a territory; most of them are bad. The odds suggest, then, that you might not be able to expect that a departing salesperson will be forthcoming or cooperative when it is time to transfer the customer notes and files. Sales force automation eliminates this concern since the system ensures that all of the relevant information is constantly available to you. If one of your salespeople gives you notice at 9 a.m., all of the important customer information can conceivably be in the hands of the new salesperson by 9:15—here is the important point—without your having to be dependent on the thoroughness or cooperation of the departing salesperson.

Security Considerations

It is right about here that a common concern about sales force automation usually arises. Sales managers, when considering the ease with which sales force automation technology moves information around, begin to wonder if sales force automation doesn't make it easier for departing salespeople to take large amounts of customer information with them when they leave. The answer to this question is, "Perhaps, but what difference does it make?" Let me explain.

It is true that, for the salesperson who is determined to leave your employ with a complete set of customer files, sales force automation might make it somewhat easier to do so. But consider the fact that this salesperson has access to no more data than he or she would otherwise. (Virtually every system can limit a salesperson's access to only his own accounts.) For the underhanded salesperson, sales force automation merely saves him or her the trouble of spending an afternoon at the copy machine. This type of individual will leave with your customer files one way or another. If a salesperson is truly determined to steal your customer files, it is almost impossible to defend yourself from such a theft, regardless of the format in which those files exist. The primary difference between an automated sales system and a manual one is the format of the stolen information, then, not one of any additional exposure to theft.

Retaining Prospects Who Are "In Process"

Stolen customer data is not the greatest risk you face when a salesperson leaves your company. The loss of existing customers is not a danger; in fact, statistics indicate that you will retain the majority of your existing customers for at least a period of time, even if you handle a transition between salespeople slowly.

A number of factors, including simple inertia on the part of the customer, will usually allow you to steal enough time to repair most, if not all, of the damage done during even a abysmally executed handoff. Even though your records might be incomplete, your company will usually have access to enough information to

> Let's say that a salesperson's quota is a million dollars a year. If you put a new person in that territory, it might normally take six months for that person to get up to speed. If you factor back in the business that you might get anyway, maybe you could assume that you're going to lose $300,000 because of the turnover. Well, if you can cut that ramp up time down to a week instead of six months, you get an immediate payback on your system.
>
> GARY ENGEL
> *John Fluke Manufacturing Company*

undertake some form of damage control. In a worst-case scenario, customer records can be at least partially reconstructed from information that should exist in your accounting department, particularly old invoices. Also, at most companies, even when the salesperson represents the primary point of contact between the customer and the company, there are usually other individuals scattered around the company who can help you and/or the new salesperson to "fill in the blanks."

None of this is possible, however, in the case of the departed salesperson's prospects who have not yet purchased anything from your company. At most companies, these potential customers are a resource that is lost forever, even though there might have already been a substantial investment involved. That investment represents the time and money spent on identifying the prospects, making initial contact, and, often, making one or more in-person sales calls.

A sales force automation system captures prospect information as readily, easily, and completely as it captures information on existing customers. See Figure 7-1. Your prospects who are in process can be retained when the salesperson who has been working with them leaves the company. Just like your existing customers, your company's sales prospects can experience a high degree of continuity in the midst of turnover in your sales department.

Two important things happen as a result of your ability to do this. First, your investment in those prospects is protected and preserved. These potential customers retain their place in the

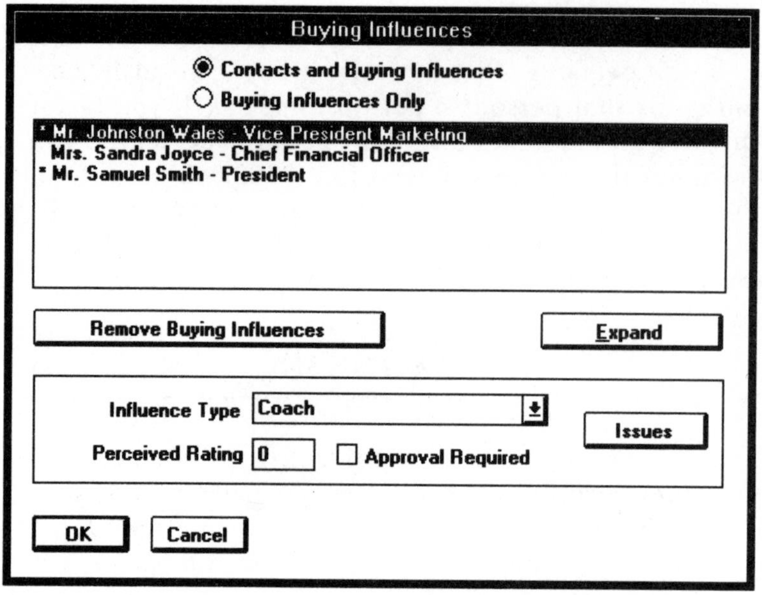

Figure 7-1. Who's Who? When a salesperson leaves, it is important to know who the key contacts are in each account. This is particularly crucial for prospects in the middle of the sales process. In this example, we see all the buying influences in a particular account. *(Copyright © 1983–1993 Sales Technologies, Inc. All rights reserved.)*

sales cycle and can be converted by your new salesperson into customers at a rate that is almost identical to that which would have occurred had your sales staff remained unchanged.

In addition, the manner in which your company is perceived by a potential customer to handle itself in the face of sales turnover can make a powerful statement about your company's ability to perform for its customers. When a problem occurs during the sales process, it is extremely difficult to make the case to your prospect that your company will perform better after the sale is made than it did before the sale was made. On the other hand, it can be extremely impressive to a potential customer to see that your company's sales management, as well as the new salesperson assigned to the account, are able to pick up the sale exactly where it was left off by the departed salesperson.

In this sense, a sales force automation system can be a tremendous marketing tool for your company. It can demonstrate your company's commitment to its customers' satisfaction. More importantly, though, it shows that you have the ability to translate that commitment into action.

When a salesperson leaves your company, he or she can leave a void that is tremendously costly in terms of lost revenue and customer satisfaction. Sales force automation gives you a set of tools that can not only minimize the damage that occurs, but can also allow you to turn a potentially negative situation into a demonstration of your company's ability to deliver the goods no matter what happens.

Summary

One of the most valuable assets in your entire company is the information that is in the possession of your salespeople about your customers. Sales force automation allows you to make certain that you have access to that information under any circumstances. It also allows you to use that information in a way that ensures continuity of service for your customers in the event that a salesperson leaves your employ.

8

Managing the Sales Process

Sales management, most sales managers would agree, is part art and part science. The art of sales management consists of insight into human nature and motivation and sensitivity to the needs of your salespeople, knowing when to cajole, when to praise, when to push, and when to back off. Dealing with these "artistic" aspects of sales management is beyond the scope of this book. There is a great deal, however, that can be said about the scientific or technical aspects of sales management. In particular, there are some important points that need to be made about how sales force automation technology provides important tools for sales managers to control those aspects. In fact, for most sales managers, this could very well be the most important chapter in this book.

We will begin by discussing a fundamental point: A primary determining factor for success in sales is the activity level of salespeople. In other words, sales is a numbers game. Of course, it is true that in any sales force there will be varying skill levels, and there will always by some salespeople who are better than others.

But when we say that one salesperson is better than another, what we are really saying is that that individual's percentages are better, that his or her close ratio is better, that his or her average sale is larger. There is no salesperson who is so terrible that he or she cannot sell anything; there is no salesperson who is so good that he or she does not strike out periodically. It is all a question of numbers.

Successful Managers Manage the Process

Although it is true that every customer and every salesperson is different and that the number of sales calls that salespeople should be making each week varies dramatically from industry to industry, and even from company to company within the same industry, ultimately, there is a set of standards that your salespeople must meet. A large part of your responsibility, as a sales manager, is to monitor the extent to which each of your salespeople is conforming to certain standards. Numbers form the basis for much of what the sales manager does.

This is not, of course, a new concept. Articles and books on sales from 70 years ago discuss this same principle. Many sales managers refer to this as managing the "sales funnel," or the "prospect backlog." As a practical matter, though, very few sales managers are able to effectively manage the activity levels of their salespeople. And this is true in spite of the fact that activity levels are the single most accurate predictor of long-term sales success. What is the problem?

The answer to that question is simple. Collecting and compiling the necessary information is usually too time-consuming and too difficult for most sales managers. For one thing, most salespeople vigorously resist the effort to collect this information. One reason for this was discussed in Chapter 3, where we saw that this type of reporting is regarded by salespeople as administrative in nature and, therefore, nonproductive. Another reason that many salespeople resist activity reporting is that, because of their independent nature, they regard management's monitoring of their activity levels as intrusive, smacking of Big Brother looking over their shoulders.

Even when the raw data is available, many sales managers do not take the time and trouble to compile it into a useful format. In fact, there are some sales managers who collect activity reports and call reports only because they know that doing so is expected of them. These managers rarely look at those reports once they are submitted. That is a self-defeating practice for a variety of reasons, but for our purposes here, I will merely note that a sales manager can only work the numbers when he or she knows the numbers.

In order to know what is going on in the sales department it is necessary to have a handle on the numbers. In fact, as a sales manager, it is impossible to do your job effectively if you do not know the numbers. In particular, you ought to have a clear understanding of:

- How many customer contacts each of your salespeople is making each week
- How many new prospects are discovered and contacted each week
- How many proposals for new business are generated each week
- How many total proposals are outstanding for each salesperson at any given time
- The dollar amounts of all outstanding proposals
- The anticipated close date of each outstanding proposal

Working the Numbers

Sales force automation technology eliminates the need for managers to manually compile the information that is necessary for them to function effectively. A sales force automation system automatically compiles activity reports that are far more detailed, and far more useful, than what is possible in a manual system. All of the numbers you will need to successfully manage the sales process are readily available through a sales force automation system. Sales force automation software can automatically produce detailed sales forecasts (see Figure 8-1). Sales force automation gives you the ability to easily look at your customers and/or prospects according to any criteria you might choose (see Figure 8-2).

Data File SAMPLE   Printed: 11/05/1992

Company Name	Forecast Date	Amount	%	Weighted Forecast
The Stevenson Company	03/28/92	$2,000.00	70	$1,400.00
The Stevenson Company	03/28/92	$8,000.00	70	$5,600.00
The Stevenson Company	03/28/92	$2,000.00	70	$1,400.00
Maxwan Corporation	03/30/92	$2,000.00	50	$1,000.00
Johnson and Murcheson	04/11/92	$2,500.00	65	$1,625.00
Johnson and Murcheson	04/11/92	$3,000.00	65	$1,950.00
Johnson and Murcheson	04/11/92	$10,000.00	65	$6,500.00
Stealth Consulting	04/12/92	$10,000.00	50	$5,000.00
Stealth Consulting	04/12/92	$6,000.00	50	$3,000.00
Stealth Consulting	04/12/92	$1,000.00	50	$500.00
Stealth Consulting	04/12/92	$1,000.00	50	$500.00
State Realty	09/05/92	$6,000.00	80	$4,800.00
State Realty	09/05/92	$4,000.00	80	$3,200.00
		$57,500.00		$36,475.00

Figure 8-1. Forecast Reports. This forecast shows the date when each sale is expected to close, as well as its probability. The ready availability of information like this is a tremendous tool; the fact that it can be produced without taking any of your salesperson's time is a bonus. *(Copyright © 1983–1993 Sales Technologies, Inc. All rights reserved.)*

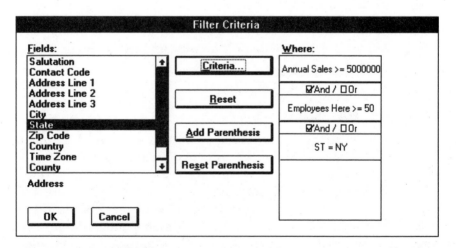

Figure 8-2. What's Going On Out There? Here, the software is "filtering" the customer file in order to find all customers who have annual sales greater than $5 million, have more than 50 employees, and are located in the state of New York. *(Copyright © 1983–1993 Sales Technologies, Inc. All rights reserved.)*

Sales automation systems can help sales managers become more effective in monitoring performance. Many sales performance problems can be directly attributed to activity deficiencies. Some cannot. In addressing a problem situation, it is first of all necessary to know which type of situation you are encountering. You cannot know this unless you have a grasp of the numbers involved. Is a problem salesperson making more or fewer calls than his or her more successful colleagues? Does he or she have more proposals outstanding or fewer?

Not only is it necessary to know this information but, if you are going to be an effective coach or counselor for a problem sales person, you must be able to establish your credibility in an authoritative and objective manner. Once again, having access to the numbers will make the difference. It is far less effective to tell a salesperson that you do not think that he or she is making enough sales calls than it is to point out that he or she is making five fewer calls per week, on average, than the rest of the sales team. Sales force automation will give you the information and, hence, the credibility you need. See Figure 8-3.

Closing the Loop on Sales Leads

Closely related to the question of activity management is the issue of managing sales leads. Most companies invest large amounts of marketing dollars for the purpose of generating sales leads. And, as most salespeople and sales managers know, a great deal of that money is wasted.

The unfortunate reality is that, except in those instances where sales leads generated by the marketing department represent the majority of a company's prospecting efforts, sales leads usually receive inadequate follow-up. Salespeople often regard the follow-up of these leads as a low-priority activity that seldom produces enough results to justify the effort. This is exacerbated by the fact that sales managers do not maintain their focus on the follow-up of sales leads for a period of time that is long enough to make a difference. As a result, the leads get collected, are held by a salesperson for a while, and then, ultimately, get discarded.

```
┌──────────────────────────────────────────────────────────────────┐
│ ────── MIKE's Forecasted Sales Window ──────                       │
├────────────────────────────────────────────────────────────────┬─┤
│ Choose  Zoom  Sort  Analysis  User  Edit  Delete  Top  Bottom  Quit│
├───────────┬───┬──────────┬────────────────────┬───────────────────┤
│ Close Date│ % │ Forecast │ Product            │ Company           │
├───────────┼───┼──────────┼────────────────────┼───────────────────┤
│ Sep  6, 91│ 80│  45,000  │ 200+ ColdMine single│ Richard Weed,  Ern│
│ Sep 10, 91│ 90│     500  │ Single User ColdMine │ Janet Jones,  Jenn│
│ Sep 16, 91│ 80│   1,400  │ Network ColdMine    │ Sam Perkins,  Samu│
│ Oct  1, 91│ 95│   7,500  │ 25 Single User GoldMi│ Cindy Brush,  Josh│
│ Oct 17, 91│ 85│     895  │ Network ColdMine    │ Andrew Walther,  A │
│ Nov  1, 91│ 75│  75,000  │ 100 User Site Lic.  │ Bud Meyer,  Southe │
├───────────┴───┴──────────┴────────────────────┴───────────────────┤
│ Last Contact: n/a      Last Attempt: n/a        Open:              │
│ ≡&=»  Time:            Time:                     Open:             │
├────────────────────────────────────────────────────────────────── │
│ (vF)         │      File: Common Contact File   │ Wed Feb 17  2:15p│
└────────────────────────────────────────────────────────────────────┘
```

```
┌──────────────────────────────────────────────────────────────────┐
│ ────── MIKE's Forecasted Sales Analysis ──────                     │
├─────────────────┬───────────┬────────────┬──────────┬─────────────┤
│     Period      │ # of Sales│ Forecasted │ % Prob.  │  Potential  │
├─────────────────┼───────────┼────────────┼──────────┼─────────────┤
│ Sep 2  - Sep 8 :│     1     │   45,000   │  88.00   │   36,000    │
│ Sep 9  - Sep 15:│     1     │      500   │  90.00   │      522    │
│ Sep 16 - Sep 22:│     1     │    1,400   │  80.00   │    1,120    │
│ Sep 23 - Sep 29:│     0     │        0   │   0.00   │        0    │
│                 │           │            │          │             │
│  Next 4 Weeks:  │     3     │   46,900   │  80.12   │   37,642    │
├─────────────────┼───────────┼────────────┼──────────┼─────────────┤
│ September, 1991: │     3     │   46,900   │  80.12   │   37,642    │
│ October, 1991:   │     2     │    8,395   │  93.93   │    7,886    │
│ November, 1991:  │     1     │   75,000   │  75.00   │   56,250    │
│ December, 1991:  │     0     │        0   │   0.00   │        0    │
│      Beyond:     │     0     │        0   │   0.00   │        0    │
│                  │           │            │          │             │
│  Total Forecast: │     6     │  130,375   │  78.07   │  101,778    │
├──────────────────┴───────────┴────────────┴──────────┴─────────────┤
│ ────── Press any Key to Continue ──────                            │
│ (vfA)        │      File: Common Contact File   │ Mon Sep 2  2:16p │
└────────────────────────────────────────────────────────────────────┘
```

Figure 8-3. No Surprises. This report analyzes one salesperson's projected sales on a weekly basis for each of the next four weeks, and on a monthly basis for each of the next four months. The information can be consolidated for a sales team, for a region, or for an entire company. Sales force automation can make sales forecasting not only easier but also more effective. (*Courtesy of Elan Software.*)

Still, the marketing department keeps the bingo cards rolling in.

Now, there are two possibilities in this situation, and they are mutually exclusive. One possibility is that salespeople and sales managers are squandering a valuable resource by neglecting the leads that are supplied to them. The other possibility is that the salespeople are right, the leads are worthless, and the marketing department is wasting a tremendous amount of money. Of course, I have no way of knowing which of these alternatives is true at your company, but I can tell you that it would be a good thing for you and the marketing department to find out! I can also tell you that you will never know the answer with any degree of certainty until a system is established that closes the loop on sales leads. In other words, you ought to be able to tell how many sales leads were generated in a period of time, where those leads went, how many of them closed, and how much revenue was generated by them.

> With a manual system, you can run a promotion, get a response from a potential customer, send it out to the sales force, and you never know what happened to it. There is no reliable feedback mechanism in a manual system. Also, the world is moving toward extremely targeted marketing. Companies are becoming more and more targeted, aiming a specific message at a specific group of prospects. You just cannot do that without sales force automation.
>
> JOHN POST
> *Hewlett-Packard*

Most sales managers understand this, but find themselves confronted with the same problem they face when dealing with the tracking of salespeoples' activity levels: In the real world, collecting and compiling the necessary information is too time consuming and too difficult.

Once again, sales force automation provides a solution. A sales force automation system, by design, does not allow anything to fall through the cracks. And, as we saw with activity monitoring, the system automatically compiles the information that is necessary for the sales manager to function effectively. See Figures 8-4 and 8-5.

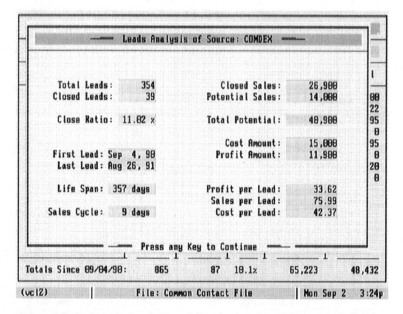

Figure 8-4. Lead Analysis. Sales force automation can help you "close the loop" on sales leads, targeting your marketing dollars more effectively because you can monitor results. *(Courtesy of Elan Software.)*

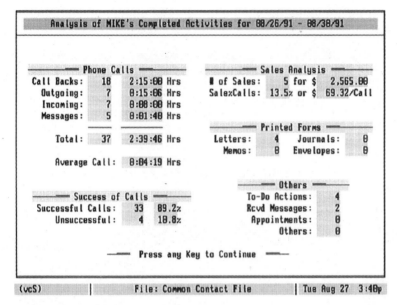

```
┌─────────────────────────────────────────────────────────────┐
│    Analysis of MIKE's Completed Activities for 88/26/91 - 88/38/91 │
│                                                               │
│   ─────── Phone Calls ───────      ──────── Sales Analysis ───────── │
│   Call Backs:   18   2:15:88 Hrs    # of Sales:    5 for $  2,565.88 │
│    Outgoing:     7   8:15:86 Hrs   SalesCalls:  13.5% or $  69.32/Call │
│    Incoming:     7   8:88:88 Hrs                              │
│    Messages:     5   8:81:48 Hrs                              │
│                                      ──────── Printed Forms ──────── │
│      Total:     37   2:39:46 Hrs    Letters:   4   Journals:     8 │
│                                      Memos:     8   Envelopes:   8 │
│      Average Call:   8:84:19 Hrs                              │
│                                                               │
│                                       ──────── Others ──────── │
│    ─────── Success of Calls ───────   To-Do Actions:    4 │
│   Successful Calls:   33   89.2%      Rcvd Messages:    2 │
│      Unsuccessful:     4   18.8%      Appointments:     8 │
│                                           Others:       8 │
│                                                               │
│              ─────── Press any Key to Continue ─────── │
│                                                               │
│  (vcS)          │      File: Common Contact File      │ Tue Aug 27  3:48p │
└─────────────────────────────────────────────────────────────┘
```

Figure 8-5. Working the Numbers. Sales force automation software can automatically compile activity data, making it easier for sales managers to pinpoint problem areas that could be improved. The burden of activity reporting can be lifted from salespeople; at the same time, sales managers can have access to better information! *(Courtesy of Elan Software.)*

Sales leads can be entered into a sales automation system by the salesperson when the lead is assigned by a sales manager. A more effective method, however, would be for all sales leads to be entered into the system at the time they are generated (perhaps by staff from marketing), and then assigned out by the sales manager directly from the system. Regardless of how the leads are entered into the system, they can be identified with their source. This would allow you to track leads that were generated from a trade show separately from leads that came in response to advertising.

The important point, though, is the fact that once a lead is entered into the system, it stays there until there is some final disposition. This allows you to know exactly what is happening with each lead. It also allows you to gather valuable information. You might find out that:

- The leads from your West Coast trade show generated $500,000 worth of business, while the Midwest trade show only generated $28,000.

- Customers that resulted from a newspaper advertising campaign last month made purchases that were 20 percent greater than the company's average invoice.

- Sales leads that were followed up by your salespeople within three business days turned out to be three times more productive than leads that were not followed up for a week or more.

All of this is potentially valuable information. It allows your marketing department to make the most effective use of its resources. It also gives you the tools to make certain that potential customers are not overlooked.

Getting Close to Your Customers

Another related benefit of a sales automation system is that the data automatically collected helps you to examine and understand sales trends and tendencies. Moreover, not only does sales automation give you the ability to do this easily, but it also allows you to do it on an ad hoc basis, so that the information that you are working with is current. The advantage of automation is that you as a sales manager can have access to the information while it is still timely enough to do you some good!

A sales representative can really only call on approximately 140 physicians per month, so it is important to target the market by physician specialty and physician productivity. We know that approximately 25 percent of physicians generate 75 to 80 percent of our business in any given territory, so it is critical to identify and impact that segment of the market. Automation makes this much easier.

GEORGE ZORBAS
Lederle Labs

For the past two decades, as large computer systems have become entrenched in corporate America, sales managers have been inundated with huge amounts of raw data, often in the form of voluminous computer printouts. While the objective behind providing this information is laudable, two problems have traditionally resulted. The first is that the data has not been in a format in which it is useful to the average sales manager. The second problem is that the data usually takes far too long to reach its destination. It provides an interesting historical record, perhaps, but it is not a tool with which a manager can do his or her job.

> I think that with a manual system, there was a tendency to only record the most important information. We have more information about our markets now and about our customers. I think we are getting a better understanding of our customers.
>
> WILLIAM FRIEL
> *Goodyear Tire and Rubber*

These problems are eliminated with a well-designed sales automation system. Captured sales information can be graphed, charted, or plotted on a map (see Figure 8-6). In this way, reams of raw data are distilled into an easily understandable format. More important, though, is the fact that a sales automation system gives a sales manager instant, real-time access to information. If sales of a particular product are tailing off in a certain territory, it is important to know this right away. Similarly, if there is a surge in product sales in a certain area, or among a certain group of customers, being able to spot the trend while it is happening allows you to react to it and to capitalize on opportunities that the marketplace presents.

It is important to note here that most sales software allows sales managers to dig into the sales data in an ad hoc fashion. Unlike computer reports that are generated at the home office, a sales automation system gives you the power to view the data in any way that you like, to "slice it up" in whatever manner will be most useful at a given time. Your flexibility and your ability to be responsive to market conditions that can change at a blinding pace are tremendously increased.

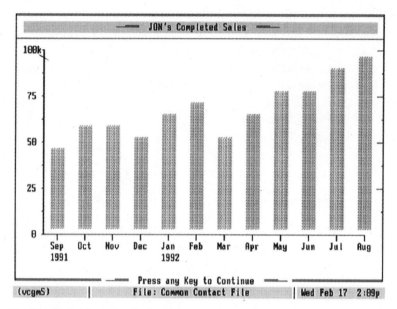

Figure 8-6. Graphic Information. Most sales force automation software will allow you to examine important information in a graphic format. This makes the information easier to understand; it also allows managers to identify trends or problems more quickly. *(Courtesy of Elan Software.)*

Account Management

In working with hundreds of sales managers over the years, I have observed that many sales managers find their most complex challenges, as well as their largest opportunities, in the area of large account management. For the purpose of this discussion, we can define the term "large account" broadly. For some companies, their large account opportunities will be primarily local; for others, they might be national or even international in scope. In all cases, though, a large account is defined as one that represents a major sales opportunity for your company. It will also be characterized by one or more of the following:

- More than one of your salespeople calling on the account
- A customer that has several locations that purchase independently, even though all the purchasing might be done under a blanket agreement

- Multiple customer sites that require service
- The involvement of several of your company's branch offices or locations

The theme that is common throughout all of these defining characteristics is one of complexity. A maze of people and locations—your customer's and yours—must be negotiated in a way that allows you to meet the needs of your customer. And, of course, this must be done in a way that is profitable even in the face of the typically low profit margins that are characteristic of the large account environment.

Your responsibility is to coordinate the entire picture, deploying your company's resources effectively within the context of a structure that is defined by your customer. Any attempt to require your customer to accommodate your structure is likely to result in dissatisfaction on the part of your customer and, in time, will almost certainly cause you to lose the business. If your customer wants each branch location to generate its own orders then that is how you must respond. If another customer wants all ordering centralized, you need to be able to adapt to that situation as well.

Communication Is the Key

The foundation of any successful account management scenario is a fast, responsive communications structure. (In Chapter 10, we discuss the general impact of the improved communications that results from the implementation of a sales force automation system in your sales department. Right now, however, we will focus on the impact that computer communications has on account management.)

Regardless of how your large account wants its selling situation structured, it is important that everyone involved in the management and servicing of the account—particularly you, the sales manager in charge of the entire operation—have timely access to necessary information. If there are several salespeople calling on different branches of the account, those activities must be coordinated. If there is an account manager involved, that individual must know what is taking place with every salesperson, at every branch location.

It is the sales manager's responsibility to create the mecha-
nisms that allow for the proper communication of information
around the company. In situations where all of the people
involved have physical access to each other regularly, hallway conversations can fill in some of the blanks. (Even when that kind of
access is possible, it should also be pointed out that it is not
always the best way to address the requirements of the situation.
Hallway conversations are less likely to receive adequate follow-
up than more formal communications.)

Sales Team Selling

In most situations, however, the logistics do not provide for that
kind of informal access. It is more likely that salespeople who
share responsibility for an account are located in different offices,
often in different states. In those instances, the electronic communications that a sales automation system can provide is far superior
to any other tool that might be used to solve the problem.

> In a team selling situation where three or more people might
> be calling on an account, the last thing you need is for people
> to be inconsistent. The ability to share information through
> computer technology has really extended the notion of team
> selling. You can have sort of a virtual team even among people
> in different time zones and thousands of miles apart.
>
> KEVIN FLYNN
> *Apple Computer*

Used in this way, a sales force automation system allows management to create a cohesive sales team, even though that team is
composed of individuals who are separated from each other by
thousands of miles. When members of your sales team are communicating efficiently with each other, the interests of your customers are served as well, since your team is better able to meet
the customer's needs. From your standpoint as a manager, better
communications will also lead to more accurate forecasting, as
well as better information about what is going on in the account.

And, as we saw in Chapter 7, sales force automation will help you to provide your large account customers with a high degree of continuity of service, regardless of what happens with any individual member of your sales team.

Managing communications, like managing the numbers, is part of the overall management challenge of managing the sales process. Sales force automation enhances your capabilities in every aspect of that process.

Summary

The sales process at many companies involves a fairly standard, identifiable sequence of events. An important element of a sales manager's success is his or her ability to monitor those events and to make certain that salespeople are engaging in the appropriate activities.

Sales force automation provides managers with a set of tools that makes it easy and convenient for them to manage the sales process.

9

How to Painlessly Reduce the Costs of Selling

Sales managers have an understandable tendency to focus their attention on driving sales and generating revenue. It is naturally more exciting and glamorous to concentrate on achieving a record sales month than it is to devote a comparable amount of effort on lowering the cost of sales. But glamorous or not, cost containment is an important part of every manager's job, particularly in today's hypercompetitive business environment.

Lower the Costs of Selling

The sales department is fertile ground for cost containment efforts. Widely accepted industry figures indicate that the sales and marketing department can account for up to 35 percent of the total budget of the average corporation. And, like so many other costs of doing business, the cost of selling is skyrocketing.

In 1990, it was estimated by the Harvard Business Review that the average cost of a sales call in the computer industry was $300 per hour! When you consider these facts along with our observation in Chapter 2 that the sales departments of most companies tend to be the last areas in the corporation to experience any of the benefits of computer technology, it becomes clear that opportunities exist to dramatically lower the cost of sales. And, given the fact that sales costs account for a large portion of most companies' overall costs, the impact of lowered selling costs can be significant.

Make Fewer Sales Calls

The introduction of sales force automation can impact selling costs in a number of ways. As we saw in Chapter 3, Storage Technology found that their sales automation system helped them to decrease the average number of sales calls that it took to close a sale by 20 percent. Such a dramatic improvement is not uncommon. Although your company's cost of sales might not quite reach the $300 per hour level of the computer industry, the fact is that a 20 percent decrease in the number of sales calls that are necessary in order to close the sale is bound to be significant.

There are several reasons that sales force automation has this kind of impact. The most important is that a well-designed sales automation system puts more usable information into the hands of salespeople. As a result, salespeople can greatly reduce the number of times that it is necessary to have to get back to the customer with answers to questions or other information that the customer might request.

Similarly, a sales automation system can allow a salesperson to develop a complete proposal for a customer on the spot instead of having to go back to the office to do so. This approach also allows proposals to be developed in an interactive manner. As questions arise, they can be answered immediately. If a customer, after seeing a proposal, wants to see certain variations or options, additional proposals reflecting those changes or options can be easily created right on the spot. Using this approach, a proposal process that might have required two or three sales calls can be handled in a single call.

Increase Customer Retention

The cost of selling to a new customer is approximately five times greater than the cost of selling to an established customer. Part of the reason for this is that, once you have demonstrated your value as a supplier, an existing customer does not need to be resold on the benefits of doing business with your company. Although it is never a bad idea to reemphasize some of those points, they do not need to continue to be part of the primary selling proposition every time you call on that customer.

In addition, numerous studies have indicated that an existing customer will buy more in an average order than a new customer. While the fixed costs associated with selling your product remain the same, the higher average dollar amount per sale will result in lower variable costs.

As we saw in Chapter 4, a sales force automation system can make a tremendous difference in the level of customer satisfaction that you achieve. This increased customer satisfaction will almost always translate directly into increased customer retention. And, in addition to its other obvious benefits, customer retention translates directly into lowered costs. Your overall cost of selling goes down in direct proportion to your rate of customer retention.

Sales force automation impacts customer retention at another, more fundamental level. In study after study, the most widely cited reason for customers' changing suppliers is that the existing supplier simply does not pay attention to them. This fact becomes especially troubling when you consider the results of a recent survey of over 4000 businesses which indicated that the typical salesperson had not contacted 41 percent of his or her customers during the previous calendar year; only 16 percent of sales representatives made it a point to contact every one of their accounts during that same time period. The primary reasons cited for this abysmal performance were:

- Illegible paper records
- Difficulty of going through hundreds of records to see where each account stood in the sales cycle

A sales force automation system easily eliminates these problems. It can be a critical tool to help ensure that every single one of your customers is contacted on a regular basis, thereby allowing your company to lower its cost of selling through increased customer retention.

Reduce Administrative Costs

A sales force automation system can also lower your company's cost of selling by reducing the administrative costs associated with the sales department. This happens through:

- Reduced communications costs
- Reduced paperwork
- Elimination of redundant data entry

Lower Communications Costs

Electronic mail increases the speed of communications, but it also considerably lowers the cost of communications in terms of postage and overnight services.

One large company that I studied was able to document over $100,000 in savings in just a three-month period after the introduction of an electronic mail system. This figure was the net result of the savings achieved by eliminating the distribution of paper to the field offices less the cost associated with the operation of the electronic mail system. (It should be noted that this company maintains that the *quality* of its communications also improved over the same period.)

Lower Paperwork Costs

Every time a salesperson or other employee of your company creates, transmits, or files a piece of paper, an expense is incurred. It is, of course, neither possible nor necessarily desirable to eliminate the flow of paper altogether, but there are many instances in which paper flow can be reduced or eliminated.

> A simple thing like a change in a customer's address used to have to be mailed in on paper forms, then get keyed into the system by an administrative person at headquarters. It would take days. Now, a salesperson can just make the change on the system and it gets uploaded along with all their data every day. We have eliminated a lot of paper being mailed in from the field.
>
> SAM STEINHOUSE
> *Progressive Companies*

A sales automation system can eliminate the need for a great deal of the administrative expense associated with the filing of correspondence since all correspondence can be stored electronically in the system. In addition, the cost of the actual paper that is necessary for things like copies of letters and phone messages is eliminated. While these may seem like trivial expenses, the cumulative savings can be significant. Moreover, as we have noted with other aspects of automation, the savings are achieved while the effectiveness and usability of the systems are actually improved.

Eliminate Redundant Data Entry

It is dismaying to consider how much time and money we spend on the unnecessary duplication of administrative effort. Sales orders are written up by salespeople only to be rekeyed into a computer system by a sales administrator. Expense reports are written, rewritten, and summarized by a similarly redundant effort.

Any information that is entered into a computer system is portable. In other words, when information is entered into the system once, there is no reason for it to be reentered. As a result, a great deal of time (and, therefore, money) is saved by eliminating unnecessary administrative redundancy.

Closely linked to the elimination of redundancy is the fact that a sales force automation system can also lower costs by maintaining cleaner data in the system. Since a great deal of data maintenance is done by salespeople who are close to the field, the data

> We found that our salespeople's mailing lists became a great
> deal cleaner. The salespeople could work with their lists and
> tell if the addresses were all screwed up or were not current
> anymore. They were able to immediately clean them up. As a
> result, when we sent out our catalogs, which are fairly expen-
> sive, we did not get as many returns. That's an expense you
> can easily put a number on.
>
> GARY ENGEL
> *John Fluke Manufacturing Company*

that is found in a sales automation system tends to be cleaner
and more current that what is found in a typical marketing database. As a result, marketing expenses are not incurred on customers who have moved, went bankrupt, or died. A cleaner database means that marketing dollars are not wasted.

Reduce Training Expenses

The best sales managers devote a large part of their overall bud-
gets to making certain that their salespeople are well trained.
Training salespeople is an expenditure that can truly be considered an investment, not in the doublespeak sense that politicians
and others use when they really mean "cost," but rather in the
sense of an investment that produces a real, quantifiable return.
A well-trained sales force is demonstratably more productive,
generating more gross revenue and better gross margins. In addition, many independent studies have verified the fact that companies that invest in the training of their salespeople experience
less costly turnover than companies that do not.

> There is no question about it that it is much easier to train
> someone when you have a standard set of tools. Having the
> thing on a computer really makes it much easier.
>
> RON MENZEL
> *Holmes Protection*

Recognizing these facts, it is not my intention to argue against the need for training or even to necessarily argue that training expenses are too high. Rather, I am suggesting that training expenses, like other expenses, should be kept as low as possible consistent with the achievement of the desired results.

Generally speaking, training that is given to salespeople falls into one of three categories:

1. Sales training (the principles and techniques involved in prospecting, qualifying, presenting, and closing sales)
2. Product training (the features, benefits, and competitive positioning of the company's products)
3. Policy and procedure training (how to function administratively within the company)

Although there are a few instances of training in sales techniques being conducted in a computer-based format, this is the exception rather than the rule. Training in the first category still tends to be best when it is done in person. It is in the latter two categories of training that sales force automation tends to be most effective.

Product Training

Most companies introduce new products regularly. It is naturally necessary to make certain that salespeople are familiar with these new products so that they can sell them effectively. In the past, companies have undertaken this type of training by sending trainers out to the field or, alternatively, bringing salespeople to a centralized training facility to be trained. Many of these companies have found that interactive, computer-based training modules are as effective as the training methods that have been used in the past. The difference is that interactive computer-based training can be conducted at a fraction of the cost of other types of training.

One high-tech company that I studied was able to document over one million dollars worth of savings by moving to a computer-based training structure for new-product training. This savings was accomplished with no measurable difference in the thoroughness or effectiveness of the training. Most companies will not be able to generate savings that are this dramatic, but will, nevertheless, be able to make meaningful improvements in the cost structure of new-product training.

Policy and Procedure Training

The greatest benefit of a sales force automation system has to do with training in policies and procedures. A sales force automation system creates a structure that makes training these areas easier and less time-consuming. The reason for this is straightforward. In a comprehensive, integrated system, all of the administrative components of the salesperson's job are included in the system. As a result, administrative tasks, such as call reports and expense reports, require virtually no additional training.

> Before we automated, it sometimes took six months for a new salesperson to become productive. Now, with the structure that the system provides, as well as the ease of getting to the information, we have had people tell us that they're up and running in five days. The territory is analyzed by zip code or by some other criteria and the forecast is relatively easy to produce. The new salesperson is confident and can be productive right away.
>
> GARY ENGEL
> *John Fluke Manufacturing Company*

Training New Salespeople

Another important plus of sales force automation is that an automated system allows a sales manager to plug a new salesperson right into an open territory. Then, using the system, the manager can assign activities, monitor those activities, and even engage in a certain amount of coaching via electronic mail. The details will vary from company to company, but the principle remains the same. A sales force automation system can provide a structure that allows new salespeople to become productive much more quickly than they possibly could otherwise.

Finally, it should be noted that companies that do not have automated sales systems might lose out in recruiting the best new salespeople. There are indications that quality sales trainees are beginning to look for companies that have automated sales system, and are dismissing out of hand the prospect of working for those companies that have not yet done so.

This is a predictable trend, one that has already been noted in numerous business publications. As the use of computers becomes a standard element in all levels of education, it is likely that this expectation will become even more universal. And, in any discussion of lowering costs, it is clear that not being able to recruit the best sales talent available is, in the long run, one of the highest costs of all.

Summary

Profitability is enhanced not only by the ability to increase sales but also by the ability to eliminate unnecessary costs and to increase operational efficiencies. Sales automation technology allows sales managers to drive unnecessary costs out of their sales operations without sacrificing sales productivity.

10

Communications— The Essence of Sales Force Automation

When the uninitiated think of sales force automation, there is a tendency to view the subject strictly in terms of the function of contact management. While it is true that contact management is generally regarded as the *sine qua non* of sales force automation, it is also true that the most profound benefits of implementing a sales automation system are often realized in other areas.

During the course of interviewing dozens of executives for this book, I had the opportunity to review the results of a variety of different approaches taken by sales managers who undertook to automate their sales operations. More important, as I interviewed these managers, I was able to question them on the aspects of their automation efforts that yielded the greatest return on their investment. One theme emerged with a regularity that was surprising to me at first. As I became more familiar with the issues involved, however, the point these sales managers were making became perfectly clear. It can be summarized in the words of one manager who put it very succinctly: "Every sales automation solution is, in fact, a communications solution."

> The objective is to have the information flow smoothly up and down through the company. The availability of information is really the whole show.
>
> RON MENZEL
> *Holmes Protection*

In the fast-paced business environment of the 1990s, many companies believe that their ability to manage their communications is a critical component of their success. But the ability to accurately deliver information into the hands of those who need it or who would benefit from it is not a simple undertaking. Consider how many times you have seen or been involved in misunderstandings or missed communications. Your own experience will, no doubt, indicate that communicating is challenging, even under the best of circumstances. You might be able to think of a time when you were face-to-face with a colleague or an employee, thereby being able to make use of various visual cues and verification opportunities, and still did not get the communication quite right.

Consider, then, the challenge of communicating with a field-based sales force. When you think about the problems that are inherent in the logistics of such an arrangement, it is almost surprising that any meaningful communication takes place at all. Salespeople operate on different schedules, so their availability is often an issue. Moreover, many sales managers must wrestle with the fact that their salespeople are located in different time zones, further complicating the communications picture.

Finally, there is the complexity and variety of the communication itself. Information that needs to be communicated between salespeople in the field and managers and administrative personnel in the home office includes:

- Sales orders
- Sales forecasts
- Sales call reports

- Changes in policies and procedures
- Situational updates
- Competitive information

This list is by no means complete and is not intended to be comprehensive. Its purpose is to illustrate the scope of the challenge that sales managers must address.

Some of these items are best handled in the context of a one-on-one communication between a sales manager and a salesperson. In certain instances, one or more other people in the company might also need to be included in the communications loop. Other items on the list must be made available to the entire sales department.

> Salespeople are not islands. They work best when they do not feel isolated. Even though they might be 2000 miles away, they have to feel that they are connected.
>
> KEVIN FLYNN
> *Apple Computer*

The proliferation of fax and voice mail systems has plugged up some of the holes. In fact, both have a legitimate and useful place in the overall communications scheme of most companies. However, as we review the above list of communications requirements, it is clear that even the combination of fax and voice mail is not adequate for all of the tasks that we identified. Many sales managers have come to the conclusion that only an electronic mail system can satisfy all of the varied communications requirements that are part of managing a field-based sales force.

Sales Orders

In Chapter 5, we discussed the ways in which an automated sales system could impact the sales order cycle. The important thing to remember is that the electronic transmission of sales orders is the fastest, most accurate way to move this critical information between the field and the home office.

> Salespeople used to have to submit information manually. Then a clerical person would type it up. It would be like playing "telephone" at a party—there would be 12 errors by the time you were done with it. Now we know that the data is cleaner, there is no question about that.
>
> RON MENZEL
> *Holmes Protection*

Sales Forecasts

From a sales manager's point of view, the importance of timely, accurate sales forecasts cannot be overstated. There is nothing quite as needlessly frustrating as being surprised at the month-end sales results because the forecasts from the field were incorrect, untimely, or inadequate.

More than simply keeping sales managers up to date, accurate sales forecasting can have an important impact on other areas of the company as well. Sales forecasts give management the information that is necessary to implement a product plan that ensures that the right product is available for salespeople to sell.

> One of the other benefits that we realized from the system is that we are able to much more accurately predict sales because we have the information in the computer faster about what our customers are ordering. This allows us to get our factories geared up a lot faster to build the right product rather than building the wrong product.
>
> DAVID JOY
> *Stanley Tools*

It is true that a sales force automation system cannot compensate for poor forecasting skills of salespeople in the field. What a sales system can do, however, is to move the information from the field to management instantly. Perhaps more important is the fact that an automated sales system can deliver the information in a format that allows the forecasts of several salespeople to be automatically rolled up into a consolidated regional report. Since the information is in a more usable format, it is more valuable to management. It is more likely to be useful in preventing end-of-the-month surprises.

Sales Call Reports

When the members of a sales staff are spread out over a large geographic area, sales call reports are a critical component of a sales manager's efforts to keep a finger on the pulse of what is going on in the territory.

There are, of course, a variety of means by which a sales call report can be delivered to a sales manager. Sales reports that are submitted by mail often do not arrive on a timely enough basis to allow them to be as useful as they should be. Every sales manager will, from time to time, discover in a sales call report a situation that requires, in the manager's judgment, immediate attention. Mail simply does not get there quickly enough.

It is critical for both sales and management to have a finger on the pulse on the business. This means knowing where the business is and where it isn't, and being able to analyze the situation by product, by geography, by timing. This allows everyone to do a better job at sales planning. As a manager, I want to be able to keep an eye on all of these elements more easily and to be able to monitor everything, not just from the standpoint of an evaluation, but also from the standpoint of being able to provide positive feedback.

JAMES WEGLARZ
SmithKline Diagnostics

A fax can get there more quickly, but, for a fax transmission to be timely, a sales manager must be there to receive it. Since sales managers are spending more time in the field and less time at the office, this is not always feasible.

The electronic mail component of a sales automation system is completely portable. Sales force automation allows a salesperson with a notebook computer to communicate with a similarly equipped sales manager anytime, anyplace.

Changes in Policies and Procedures

Changes in policies and procedures are typically dispatched to field-based salespeople by mail. When you consider the speed of the mail, and combine that with the fact that salespeople often spend no more than a day or two out of every week in the office, it is not uncommon for this information to take two weeks or more to reach a salesperson.

The significance of this kind of delay depends, naturally, on the nature of the information involved. The result may be that the salesperson in the field does not have the information that he or she needs to do the job. However, even less consequential delays contribute to the demoralizing feeling of isolation and disconnectedness that is so common among field-based salespeople.

> There is a lot of information—policies and procedures, competitive information, things like that—that used to get mailed out to our salespeople once a week, sometimes once a month. Now we can just download this stuff directly to the reps. It is there at their fingertips when they need it. We are expanding the information available to them to help them do their job. And, as an added benefit, there is no longer any question about whether or not they received it.
>
> SAM STEINHOUSE
> *Progressive Companies*

Electronic mail not only conveys information instantly, but it also keeps your salespeople feeling "plugged in" to what is going on in the company. They have access to information on the same real-time basis as their office-based colleagues. For any sales manager who can recall what it was like as a salesperson in the field, no further explanation of the benefits of electronic mail is necessary.

Situational Updates

This is a broad category that really is the heart of the issue. In those companies in which it has been implemented, electronic mail has quickly become a vital conduit through which information flows in both directions. It keeps salespeople in touch with the rest of the company but, perhaps even more important, it allows sales managers to keep their fingers on the pulse of what is going on in the field. Sales force automation software gives sales managers a way to keep up to date on customer issues. It also allows them to monitor outstanding issues so that nothing falls through the cracks. See Figure 10-1.

As a sales manager, the biggest benefit of automation is that it has allowed me to communicate with all the people that report to me virtually at any time. Because of the travel and geography involved, it is difficult to access them as a group or even individually at times. With this system, if I want to discuss something with my salespeople, give them an assignment, or convey information that I might get from my management, I can do that any time of the day or night. And they can access it any time of the day or night. I think that is the first thing. We really seem to have much better communications.

WILLIAM FRIEL
Goodyear Tire and Rubber

Once again, the point is clear and simple. Sales force automation is a tremendously effective means of communication between field-based salespeople and the rest of the company.

Competitive Information

Competitive information is sometimes considered to be the

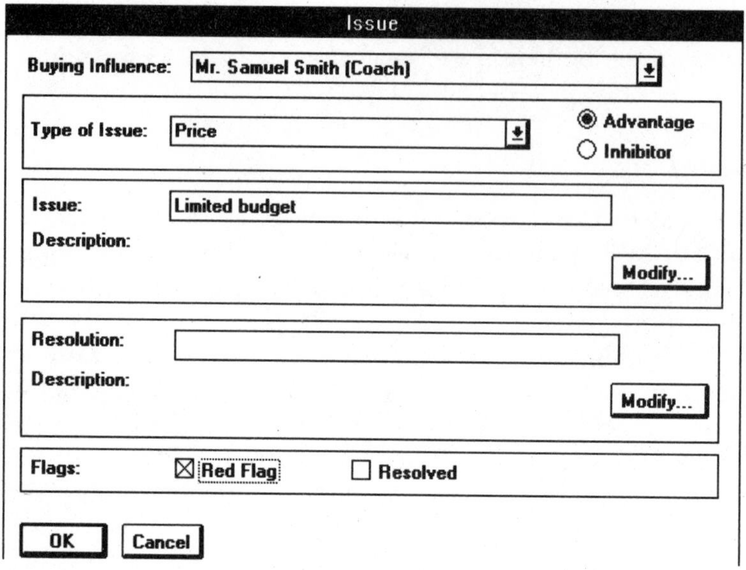

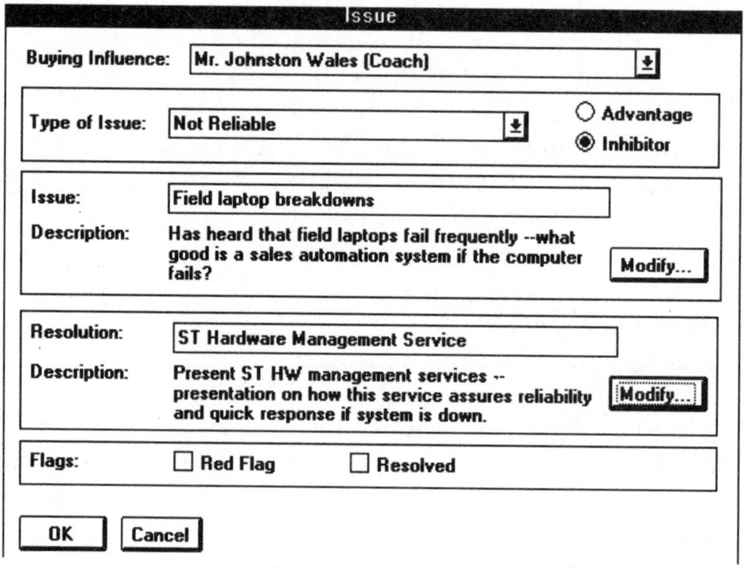

Issue

Buying Influence:	Mr. Samuel Smith (Coach) ⬇

Type of Issue: Price ⬇   ◉ Advantage
                          ○ Inhibitor

Issue: Limited budget
Description:
                                        Modify...

Resolution:
Description:
                                        Modify...

Flags: ☒ Red Flag   ☐ Resolved

OK   Cancel

Issue

Buying Influence:	Mr. Johnston Wales (Coach) ⬇

Type of Issue: Not Reliable ⬇   ○ Advantage
                               ◉ Inhibitor

Issue: Field laptop breakdowns
Description: Has heard that field laptops fail frequently --what
good is a sales automation system if the computer   Modify...
fails?

Resolution: ST Hardware Management Service
Description: Present ST HW management services --
presentation on how this service assures reliability   Modify...
and quick response if system is down.

Flags: ☐ Red Flag   ☐ Resolved

OK   Cancel

Figure 10-1. Outstanding Issues. *(Copyright © 1983–1993 Sales Technologies, Inc. All rights reserved.)*

domain of the marketing department rather than the sales department. The simple fact of the matter is that salespeople in the field are closer to the front lines of the competitive war than anyone else.

In our industry, we know that the level of marketshare that products achieve during the first six months of their introduction into the market will largely determine their share during the remainder of their life. It is not usually a gradual building process to acquire market share. Consequently, monitoring sales force activity during that period is extremely important and it helps to have information that is timely rather than historical.

GEORGE ZORBAS
Lederle Labs

While electronic mail will never supplant the more scientific measurements that are produced by the marketing department, there is often a great deal of value that management can glean from the anecdotal reports that come in from the field. This is particularly true in highly competitive situations or in situations where time is of the essence.

Summary

One of the most significant benefits of a sales force automation system is the way in which it facilitates communications among members of a sales team and between salespeople and sales management. Of all the communications technologies available to support salespeople in the field, sales force automation addresses the widest variety of needs.

This book is full of ways in which sales force automation technology can benefit salespeople and sales managers. In my judgment, the most meaningful benefit is the power of sales force automation to enhance communications, as shown in Figure 10-2.

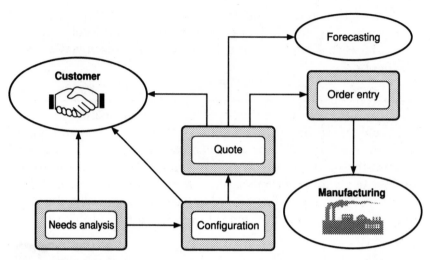

Figure 10-2. The Sales Communication System. You are competitive to the extent that you can deliver information to where it is needed quickly and accurately. *(Courtesy of Trilogy Development Group.)*

PART 4
Practical Steps in Getting Started

11

Analyzing and Understanding Your Needs

For a moment, let's forget about computer technology. We are going to spend some time thinking about your sales process. To do that, I would like to step you through an exercise that will be helpful to you immediately, regardless of when you finally undertake to automate your sales efforts.

Understand Your Manual Process First

This exercise consists of drawing a diagram of your sales process. In other words, take a piece of paper and sketch out the steps that must take place in order for you to sell your product—including as many variables as you can think of—beginning with the initial prospecting efforts and ending with the delivery of the product.

If what I am asking for is not clear, perhaps it would be helpful to look at some examples. When I was a Cub Scout, my pack launched a fund-raising drive that required us to sell boxes of cookies. Figure 11-1 is a diagram of that sales process.

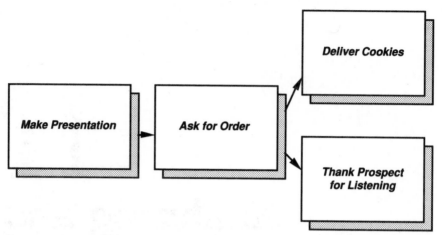

Figure 11-1. A Fairly Simple Sales Process. Selling cookies is a fairly straightforward process.

In this instance, the only variable was whether or not the prospect said yes to the sales proposition. It was not necessary to qualify prospects financially, and, since this was a one-shot deal, we did not have to be concerned with follow-up calls.

Of course, in most sales situations, the process is not that simple. The sales process for most products or services can be quite complicated. In fact, the sales process is usually based on a somewhat sophisticated model that requires attention be paid to a number of variables. Consider the diagram of a hypothetical sales process for life insurance in Figure 11-2.

One of the fallacies of sales force automation is the belief that making a large investment in software and hardware will somehow correct fundamental sales management flaws. If you automate a mess, you will merely allow your sales people to make mistakes more rapidly. If you don't have a documented sales process that everyone understands, automation means that you are going to be helter-skelter more frequently.

GIL CARGILL
IDK Group

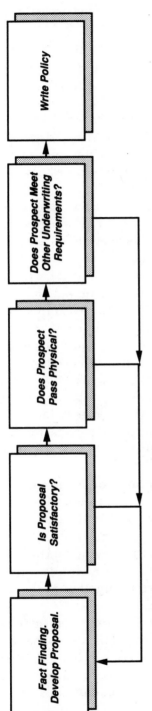

Figure 11-2. A Somewhat More Complex Sales Process. The process of selling life insurance can be complex, with several variables that need to be resolved before the sale is made.

133

Finally, add to your model some general time lines for each step in the process. Make sure that these time lines are realistic and that they reflect the everyday reality that your salespeople are actually experiencing. This is particularly important at the end of the process, after the sale is actually closed. How long does it then take to get the sales order processed and get the product delivered to your customer? If we add time lines to our previous example of life insurance sales, we wind up with the diagram in Figure 11-3.

It is an unfortunate truth that most sales managers have never attempted to diagram the sales process for their product or service. The fact is that by simply becoming more aware of what the sales process ought to look like, most managers can correct problems or make improvements. If there is a problem with a particular salesperson or account, it can be compared with the way the sales process ought to flow, as illustrated in the diagram. With this comparison, a sales manager can often diagnose a problem that might have been previously difficult to recognize. And, once diagnosed properly, of course, any problem becomes much easier to fix.

Another benefit of diagramming the sales process is that structural deficiencies in the process itself are apt to reveal themselves. More than one sales manager, after undertaking this process, has discovered that his or her salespeople are being hobbled by processes that are inherently inefficient, time-consuming, unclear, or unproductive.

So, what does all of this have to do with sales force automation? The answer is that the necessary first step in automating your sales effort is to completely understand your manual process. Applying computer technology to a process does not, by itself, make the process any better. Just as a word processor cannot turn a dime novelist into Ayn Rand, the best sales force automation system will not allow a poor sales structure to function as though it were an efficient one.

Your automated system will not necessarily mirror your manual system, but in fact, will undoubtedly give you capabilities that did not exist before, and you should not allow your existing manual system to create unnecessary or artificial constraints. However, it is necessary to know where you are before you can construct a clear picture of where you want to go.

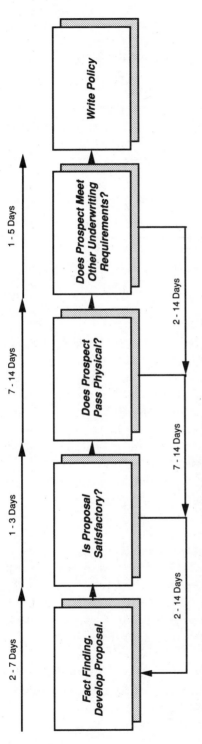

Figure 11-3. The Sales Process with Time Lines. Here general time lines have been added to the process of selling life insurance.

> I disagree with the statement "You have to have a good process before you automate it." I believe that sales force automation can create new processes, that there are things that you have never been able to do before that you can do with automation technology. You can create new ways of doing things. There are a lot of things you can do with sales force automation that you cannot do otherwise.
>
> JOHN POST
> *Hewlett-Packard*

Establish Objectives and Guidelines for Your System

Now that you have a fairly clear picture of where you are, let's start to build a model of what you want to achieve with your system, keeping in mind the general system capabilities that we discussed in Chapter 1.

Where are the areas in which you can best leverage an investment in technology? For example, your sales process model might indicate that a bottleneck exists in sales order processing. Or it might demonstrate that your sales process is particularly dependent on the ability of your salespeople to work with a large number of prospects over a long period of time. Or, if you are like most sales managers, you might find that your sales process would become more efficient if your salespeople have easier, faster access to certain pieces of information.

The answer to the question of how to best leverage your investment in sales force automation will depend on what you are selling and how you are selling it. As we have already seen, there is a wide range of approaches to the process of sales, so there are very few universal guidelines that we can identify. However, let's review examples that will give you some ideas that you can apply to your own situation.

When the ComputerLand Corporation was designing its sales force automation system, it discovered that its major customers were especially concerned with price and availability issues. Therefore, getting accurate information into the hands of a salesperson quickly was a key strategic advantage, and it became one of the cornerstones of ComputerLand's system. In addition, ComputerLand salespeople were dealing with thousands of stock keeping units (SKUs), many of which were incompatible with each other. An order that was configured improperly could lead to a return that was expensive to process. More important, though, was the fact that an incorrect order would have serious customer satisfaction ramifications, especially with large customers who were operating on tight schedules. To address this need, ComputerLand made sure that its system provided salespeople with an "electronic catalog" that included technical information.

Hewlett-Packard's Medical Products Group was in a very different situation. In building their system, they found that their leverage point was the ability to share account information among several individuals who had different responsibilities with regard to a particular customer. Salespeople needed current information on service issues; an account manager needed to be able to communicate with other salespeople who were calling on an account's field locations. The Hewlett-Packard system, then, needed to be able to manage communications in a sophisticated and intelligent manner.

A final example would be Joe De Pietro, a successful sales representative for life insurance and other financial products. Joe's communications needs are modest and relatively unsophisticated. He has found that he can best leverage his investment in sales automation by enhancing his ability to keep track of a large number of customers and prospects efficiently. For example, Joe's ability to remember a client's birthday is more than just a nice, personal touch; his being able to track birthdays and age changes accurately has a significant impact on his customers' insurance premiums as well as their ability to purchase additional coverage. Joe needed a system that could help him manage a great many details relating to an extremely large client base.

In each case, the specific leverage points, as determined by the flow of the sales process, were very different. But, in each case, sales force automation was able to address the unique requirements of the situation and contribute to a more effective sales effort.

So, where are your leverage points? What kinds of things could sales force automation do that would make a meaningful difference in the way you do business? In what ways could this technology make your salespeople more effective? Here are some ideas that you might want to consider:

- Hooking up all the salespeople in the field through an electronic mail system
- Notifying salespeople when product warranties are about to expire
- An electronic catalog of all competitive products, including features and pricing
- Producing sales agreements on the spot, with all pertinent customer information automatically filled in
- An automatic lead status report to management of leads assigned from trade show and/or advertising campaign
- Transmitting sales orders directly to your manufacturing facility from a customer's site and providing your customer with instant confirmation
- Coordinating strategy and sharing information among salespeople calling on branch offices of a large account
- Automatically generating thank-you letters after every sales call

It is not difficult to come up with a rather large list of areas that could conceivably benefit from automation, but be careful. You must make certain that you keep your focus on those areas in your business where you can truly leverage the impact of technology. In Chapter 13, we discuss this point at length, but for now, keep in mind the fact that you should apply the principle of focus to your sales force automation plan. Your project will be more successful if you use a rifle approach rather than a shotgun approach. Concentrate on your leverage points.

Map Out a Plan

You now have a fairly clear picture of what your current sales process looks like. You also have some ideas about the places in

> What we really wanted to do was to automate our sales force, give them a really simple program, one that would allow them to get out of the office more often, keep track of their clients, and also communicate with their area office or with the home office. Instead, we put fancy windows in and links to other systems, thinking this is all going to be really slick. Well, we never got to our original goal. We kept adding features. Only about 85 percent of it worked. It became such a complicated piece of logic that nobody could really follow it. We lost the confidence of a lot of our salespeople. They got really down on the system. As a result, we wound up having to backtrack.
>
> GARY ENGEL
> *John Fluke Manufacturing Company*

that process where you could most highly leverage an investment in sales force automation technology. Now, let's combine those two elements into a picture of what your sales process could look like after the introduction of sales force automation.

> The first thing that I would tell someone who is undertaking to automate their sales department is that they should have a clear understanding of what the objective is.
>
> DAVID JOY
> *Stanley Tools*

In some situations, the structure of the sales process itself will not change dramatically; the most noticeable change might be that some time lines are shortened. In other situations, the number of sales calls needed to complete a transaction might be reduced. On the extreme, you might find that the very structure of the process could change radically with the introduction of the new capabilities that sales force automation will deliver.

The point here is this: As you begin the process of building your sales force automation system, you should start with an idea of how you would like the end result to look and function. Throughout the entire process, you will want to keep these three factors in mind:

1. Customers
2. Salespeople
3. Corporate ecology

Customers

While it is true that a variety of benefits can be achieved by introducing computer technology to the sales force, you should remember that sales force automation becomes a strategic weapon only when it makes a difference to your customers, when it improves aspects of your sales process that affect the customer directly. Therefore, designing the structure of your sales force automation system should start with a look at your sales process from your customers' perspective. What information about your company and its products and services would help your customers make a better buying decision? Could that information be delivered more effectively through a sales force automation system? What about sales order information? Would making that information directly available to your salespeople in real-time at a customer site create a competitive advantage? Where are the places that automation might make your company look better and perform better for your customers? As you identify these places, use them as reference points when you design your system.

Salespeople

Your sales force automation system will only be successful to the extent that your salespeople use it. In the next chapter, we will discuss this point in depth. We will look at how to "sell" the system to sales people, how to involve them in the process, and how to use their knowledge to help you design a superior system. What I want you to keep in mind right now is that your system should be designed primarily to meet the needs of your salespeople and not to satisfy any management requirements for control or reporting. The simple reality is that management benefits flow automatically from a system that salespeople use religiously. And they will not use a system simply because management mandates that they do so. They will only use a system because it makes their job easier and makes them more productive.

Corporate Ecology

Salespeople do not function in a vacuum. They cannot sell products that manufacturing does not build. They cannot sell products to accounts that are on credit hold. There are dozens of places in your sales process that directly or indirectly involve other departments in your company. If we think of sales force automation as a tool for sharing and distributing information, then it is easy to see that much of the information involved is useful or important to departments in your company besides the sales department. And those departments usually have their own computer systems.

As you design your sales force automation system, then, you should keep in mind how it could fit into your company's overall information environment. While you can realize certain benefits even if you construct your system as an island that is unconnected to the rest of your company, it is often relatively easy to make some strategic connections to other departments that will increase the effectiveness of your system tremendously.

Vendor Selection

Now that you have designed the structure of your sales force automation system, the next step for the vast majority of companies will be selecting the software that will allow you to achieve your objectives. (A very few companies will want to seriously consider developing sales force automation software internally. I will have a few thoughts on this approach at the end of this section.) Software selection is obviously a critical piece in the puzzle of putting your system together, and it is not an easy one.

As you can see in Appendix A, there are at least 126 publishers of sales force automation software, many of whom offer several different software packages. And the appendix only lists those companies that publish sales force automation packages that are designed for a broad range of users; it does not take into consideration the software companies that have narrowed their focus to a single industry, for example, insurance sales. With so many alternatives from which to choose, how is it possible to make an intelligent selection? If you followed the process outlined above of defining the structure that you want your system to follow, you are well on your way. Here are a few additional ideas that will make your software selection process more fruitful.

Use a Consultant

There are several reputable consulting firms that specialize in the field of sales force automation. (You will find many of the best sales force automation consultants in the industry listed in Appendix B.) These consultants are familiar with many of the software packages that are available in the market, and they can offer valuable advice that will help you narrow down the list of companies that you will consider. If you follow the process described above for designing the structure of your system, and can present a consultant with the general structure that you want your system to have, you can save a great deal of time and money, since you will not need the consultant to spend a lot of time stepping you through the fundamentals.

A good consultant can also be an invaluable resource for filling in the blanks by pointing out areas that you might have overlooked in your preliminary design process. Similarly, a consultant will serve as a checkpoint for you by validating the system structure that you have designed.

At this stage in the process, your objective in working with a consultant is to come up with a list of four or five software companies that generally meet your requirements. You will want to make this objective clear to the consultant at the outset. You will find that some consultants work with just one or two software companies and will recommend those companies' products exclusively. Although this is a valid approach, one that will enable a consultant to have a much higher degree of expertise (in theory) in those packages that are his or her focus, it is not an approach that meets your needs right now. At this point in the process, your needs will better be served by a generalist rather than a specialist.

Submit a Request for Quotation

Now that you have narrowed the selection process down to a handful of software vendors, the next step in the process is to send each vendor an outline of your requirements along with a request for a proposal from them outlining the costs that would be involved in building a system, based on their software, that would meet your requirements. Make certain that you emphasize the leverage points you have identified which are unique to your sales situation and that you ask for an outline of how each vendor's product will address those specific needs.

You should include in your request for proposal any other information about your company that might be relevant. Certainly, you will want to mention:

- The number of salespeople
- The number of sales managers
- The geographic area that the new system will need to cover
- Any existing computer hardware that you will want to incorporate into the new system
- The location of any existing corporate data that the new system will need to access
- The degree of computer expertise that exists in your sales department
- The timetable that you have in mind for implementing the new system

Different sales force automation software vendors operate under very different assumptions and policies in key areas. You will want each vendor's response to address these key issues:

- Who will be responsible for the installation of the software?
- Who will train your salespeople?
- Who will be responsible for ongoing technical support for salespeople in the field?

In instances where some of these services are optional, you should request that those charges be broken out separately, rather than bundled into a single, comprehensive system price.

This approach will give you the option of exploring other alternatives for things like technical support or training in the event that the software itself meets your requirements but the company's price for those optional items is not competitive.

Vendor Evaluation

In addition to how well each company responds to your particular requirements, there are other factors that you will want to consider when you make your final decision among vendors:

- Stability
- Site license policy
- Upgrade policies

Stability.   Perhaps there is a way to feel more abandoned than having the company that publishes your sales force automation software go out of business, but I am not sure what it is. Sales force automation, once implemented, is mission critical; in other words, it is an integral part of your business operation, like a reservation system is to an airline. You simply cannot afford to have the system fail for an extended period of time. Your exposure in this regard is heightened by the fact that sales force automation is a relatively new category of software with a large number of companies trying to establish themselves in the market. As a consequence, there will no doubt be a shakeout similar to those that have occurred in other hotly contested software categories.

> It is important to do an analysis of potential vendors and to go with a reputable software supplier. Make sure that your vendor has some established track record and can give you some assurances about their future viability.
>
> GEORGE ZORBAS
> *Lederle Labs*

You will also want your sales automation system to remain up to date, taking advantage of advances in software technology as they become available. For example, as we will see in Chapter 12, a large number of users who had previously been working with applications based on MS-DOS are now migrating to Windows. When it is time for you to make such a change, you will want to be able to do so easily and painlessly.

You will want to make sure that problems and questions about your system which occur two years after your system has been installed will be addressed. Also, as new developments occur in software technology, you will want to have the option of taking advantage of them. For both of these reasons, the stability of the software vendor that you choose is an important consideration.

In your vendor selection process, you ought to be asking questions about the company, its background, and its commitment to the product whose purchase you are contemplating. There are no absolute assurances in this regard, but if you pay attention to these issues, you ought to be able to avoid those vendors that are least likely to survive.

Sometimes, you will encounter a situation where there appears to be a trade-off between company stability and functionality. In those instances, I would recommend that you opt for the former over the latter. Except in those extremely rare situations where a small company offers a certain function that is simply not available anywhere else—and that function is *uniquely* able to address one of your leverage points—your long-term needs will be better served by choosing a vendor who will be around for the long haul.

Site License Policy.   Sales force automation is, by definition, a software category that almost always encompasses several users at each company where it is implemented. You will find that different software companies have vastly different policies regarding the use of their software by more than one user at a particular company. A very few companies take the draconian approach of requiring you to purchase a separate copy of their program for each user. Some companies sell their software in five or ten packs at a substantial discount off single-user pricing. Many sales force automation software companies sell their software with a site license. You pay for a single license that will allow anyone in your company to use the software. The cost of a site license is usually determined by the number of potential users in your company, although there are some software companies that take other factors into consideration.

While site license policies have a considerable impact on the cost of acquiring the product, you should keep in mind that there are important benefits in obtaining a site license. For example, a site license will usually allow you to add an additional salesperson to your staff easily with little or no cost or administrative hassle.

By the way, I do not like to get up on a soapbox, but I need to point out that under no circumstances is it ever acceptable to simply copy software without the copyright holder's knowledge or permission. Doing so is theft—pure, unadulterated, unmitigated theft.

Upgrade Policies.   Software technology improves constantly. The software package that is state of the art today can be hopelessly antiquated in a couple of years. The company that produces your software will certainly be hard at work to make regular improvements to its product. (If they are not, you have made a bad choice of vendors.) When these improvements are made, you will usually want to adopt them.

Each company has a defined set of policies that spell out how you can do so. Differences among companies in these policies can add up to a considerable difference in the overall cost of your system over its life. Therefore, you will want to know what the upgrade policies are for the software companies that you are considering. Specifically, you should ask how often the software is upgraded and what the charge for the upgrade is.

In-House Development

As I mentioned earlier, there will be a few companies who write their own software rather than use a software vendor. While it is certainly true that there are situations where this is an appropriate approach, I believe that developing a sales force automation system internally should be any company's last resort. It should only be pursued when all other possibilities have been exhausted and should engender approximately the same enthusiasm as root canal. There are several reasons for this.

- Internal development is expensive, usually several times more expensive than even the most expensive commercial solutions.
- Internally developed applications are difficult to support because the documentation is seldom complete or comprehensive.
- It is unlikely that an internally developed application will be maintained and updated as regularly as a commercial application.
- Internally developed applications generally are inferior to commercial applications in both performance and ease of use.

To be sure, there are companies who have developed outstanding systems internally (StorageTek comes to mind), but they are the exception rather than the rule.

Also, as commercially available programs develop additional features and become more refined over time, there will be less reason to consider internal development. Just as it is difficult to imagine the need to write your own word processing software or spreadsheet, it will also be difficult to justify writing your own sales force automation package.

Summary

In undertaking your sales force automation project, you should start by developing a clear understanding of your current sales process. You should then look for the places in that process that would benefit best from automation. Finally, you should develop a plan for how your automated system will function and use that plan as the basis for selecting a software vendor.

12
An Overview of Your Options

Now that we have reviewed the basic procedural model for evaluating your sales force automation requirements and selecting a software vendor, we are going to spend some time discussing the various hardware and software options from which you will be choosing. My objective is to provide you with some guidelines that will help you to sort out the dizzying range of options you will confront.

> The real reason we were able to do what we did was not the hardware. It was the software. I do not think a lot of manufacturers really understand that yet.
>
> JOHN WILLIAMS
> *Storage Technology*

Sales automation, like every other area of computerization, is primarily an issue of software, even though, as we saw in Chapter 2, the category has been driven by advances in hardware technology. Therefore, we will begin by looking at the various software options available.

Software Options

Sales force automation software, like so many other things in life, unfortunately does not readily break down into neat, well-defined pigeonholes. However, there are some broad categories of functionality that can be useful in understanding the options that are available to you. Any type of categorization like this is, of course, quite arbitrary, and the lines between categories can become somewhat blurred. With that caveat in mind, let's take a look at these categories, listed in ascending order of sophistication:

1. Personal information managers
2. Contact managers
3. Off-the-shelf sales force automation systems
4. Customizable systems
5. Custom-designed systems

Personal Information Managers

The most basic products, which we are going to examine first, are often referred to as personal information managers (PIMs). These can be further broken down into two groups.

One group of PIMs consists of software programs that are the electronic equivalent of a Rolodex. They will store the name of a contact, the contact's company, address, and phone number. Most PIMs will also allow you to keep track of a limited number of additional pieces of information that are important to you. You might want to note a contact's birthday or shoe size, for example.

These PIMs will allow you to search through your contacts, allowing you to find all your contacts who live in Arizona, for example. Your contacts can also be sorted, either in alphabetical order, by zip code, or by some other categorization (although not all PIMs allow for extensive sorting). These products will also allow you to print a set of address labels or a personal telephone directory that will fit in your appointment book. *TouchBase* by After Hours Software is an example of this type of PIM.

The other group of PIMs includes programs that function as electronic calendars, allowing you to schedule appointments, daily tasks (to-dos), and projects. These programs can notify you of an upcoming event at a predetermined interval. They can also prevent you from scheduling conflicting appointments. And, of course, you can print out a daily, weekly, or monthly calendar. *Organizer* by Lotus is one of the programs that falls into this category.

Personal information managers, as a group, tend to be extremely easy to learn and to use. They are also very fast, require only modest computer power to run, and are inexpensive. On the other hand, they have extremely limited functionality. As a result, they are simply unsuitable as a permanent solution for the vast majority of companies that are exploring sale force automation.

This does not mean, however, that PIMs are completely without value to a sales manager who is automating his or her department. PIMs can be an ideal tool for creating the kinds of prototypes and simulations that we discussed in Chapter 11. They can be an excellent means by which salespeople and sales managers can get comfortable with computer technology while they begin the process of identifying the leverage points around which their full-blown system can later be built.

Contact Managers

Contact managers are built around the same kind of basic electronic Rolodex function that is found in personal information managers. Programs in this category, though, will typically have much more robust capabilities in this area. For example, they will allow you to search through and sort your contacts extensively. They also provide for much greater latitude in customizing the types of information that you can track for a particular contact.

In this category various other capabilities are consolidated into the software to provide much greater functionality and to allow for the effortless integration of different types of information.

Two functions that are integrated into virtually every software package in this category are calendar management and word processing. The integration of calendar management allows a salesperson to schedule an appointment with a particular contact by bringing that contact's information to the screen and logging the appointment. The appointment is automatically recorded on the salesperson's calendar without having to retype the client's name or other pertinent information. Regularly occurring appointments (e.g., annual follow-up calls) can be easily scheduled. This integration works in the other direction as well. A salesperson might note an appointment on his or her calendar, hit a key, and instantly access the underlying account information in whatever level of detail is necessary.

The integration of word processing allows a salesperson to create and store the text of commonly used letters or documents (e.g., thank-you letters). These can then be personalized for a particular contact with just a few keystrokes, since the contact's name, address, and other information is already stored in the program. In addition, the program will note in your contact's record the date that the letter was sent. (It can also record telephone calls and other events that take place with your contact.)

ACT! by Contact Software International and *TeleMagic* by Remote Control Software are two of the most widely used products in this category.

The software programs in this category are not written specifically for salespeople, but can support a sales function quite well under the right circumstances. Contact managers are more expensive than PIMs, but are still extremely affordable. They usually work best for smaller groups of salespeople, or in situations where the consolidation of information is not a critical issue. These programs are often ideal for an independent, self-employed salesperson who does not need to integrate into a larger environment. In addition, they can provide an outstanding platform for prototyping and for introducing salespeople to the productivity benefits of an automated environment. In fact, many companies have found the programs in this category to be more than adequate to meet their immediate needs.

However, these programs are general tools and are not exclusively focused on the needs of salespeople. As a result, like buying a suit off the rack, there is sometimes a problem in finding the perfect fit. In addition, these programs are not well suited to consolidate and distribute information at different levels of detail to various locations.

Off-the-Shelf Sales Force Automation Systems

The programs in this category are specifically designed to meet the needs of salespeople and sales managers. It is in this category that we begin to find long-term solutions for serious sales force automation needs.

In this category, we find specialized programs that perform very specific tasks in the sales and marketing process. For example, geographic information systems like *GeoQuery* from GeoQuery Corporation fall into this category.

The functionality of off-the-shelf sales force automation systems begins at the level that we saw in contact managers, integrating contact and account management with calendar management and word processing. In addition, these programs build in some functions that are very specific to the sales process. For example, many of the programs in this category will accommodate sales forecasting. Some will also allow you to create predefined sales tactics.

But the most important characteristic of the programs in this category is that they begin to address the issue of information sharing that is so important in the sales environment. These programs are designed to distribute information among salespeople and sales managers. It is this capability that makes these programs suitable for consideration as true, long-term solutions.

These off-the-shelf systems are often reasonably priced, sometimes at an investment level that is not considerably higher than a good contact manager. It is in this category of products that most small- to medium-sized companies will find the foundation of a sales automation strategy. *GoldMine* by Elan Software is an example of an off-the-shelf sales force automation solution.

Customizable Systems

When companies reach a certain critical mass, usually around 60 salespeople or so, the level of sophistication required to share data among salespeople, sales managers, and corporate headquarters can change dramatically. (This, of course, depends on the nature of a particular company's sales cycle and its approach to account management. Some companies find that their requirements change much earlier, some a little later.) When this happens, it is necessary to look at software that is more sophisticated and more capable than off-the-shelf packages.

The software in this category is highly customizable and has extremely sophisticated capabilities to distribute information throughout an organization wherever it is needed. *SBS* by Saratoga Systems, *SalesBase* by After Hours Software, and Modatech's *Sales Force Automation System* are products that fall into this category.

The per-user investment for software in this category is noticeably higher than what is required for off-the-shelf products. This is partly due to the fact that, in addition to the cost of the software, it is almost always necessary to have either the software vendor or a qualified consultant install and customize the software to meet your company's individual requirements. In addition, because of the sophistication of these packages, the training costs are usually somewhat higher than what is required for less capable software.

The increased investment is returned to the company though extremely sophisticated communications and data synchronization capabilities as well as through the ability to coordinate the sharing of information with other departments in the corporation. (More on data synchronization below.) In fact, the software in this category can meet the needs of the most stringent and sophisticated users. For most companies with about 60 or more salespeople, the software in this category will represent the end result of their search for a comprehensive sales force automation solution.

Custom-Designed Solutions

For the overwhelming majority of the readers of this book, there is no reason to consider a custom-designed sales force automation solution. While it is true that one of the most successful sales force automation projects that I have seen (StorageTek) was custom designed, I believe that this option will become less viable as the flexibility, capability, and quality of commercially available software continue to improve.

We have already discussed this subject in Chapter 11, so I will not belabor the point here, except to note that, because of the considerable expense involved, this option will not prove to be even remotely justifiable from a financial standpoint for any but the largest companies.

Other Considerations

As you examine the capabilities of the various sales force automation software packages from which you will be choosing, there are two areas of functionality that are important enough to merit separate discussions. These areas are:

1. Network support
2. Data distribution and synchronization

As we have seen, the benefits of sales force automation are derived, primarily, from the manner in which computer technology can facilitate communications and distribute information effectively.

This being the case, these two areas go right to the heart of virtually every sales force automation project. Software that is inadequate to meet your requirements in these areas will ultimately prove to be an unsatisfactory solution regardless of how many other whiz-bang features it possesses.

Network Support

A computer network is the combination of hardware, software, and wiring that allows different computers to share resources and to communicate with each other. In the context of sales force automation, the ability to share resources (e.g., printers) is not particularly important, the ability to communicate is critical. As a result, for any company with more than one or two salespeople, any sales force automation solution must function in a network environment in order to be truly effective.

First, network support will provide electronic mail capability. As we have already seen, electronic mail by itself can significantly enhance the effectiveness of salespeople by speeding the communications process, not only between salespeople and headquarters but also among salespeople based in the field.

In addition, network support provides the basis for the various transaction support capabilities that sales force automation can provide. It is the means by which sales order information and customer history is delivered to the appropriate people and departments in a company.

Finally, network support is the foundation for the data synchronization capabilities that we will be discussing shortly.

In an office environment, network support does not present a technical or functional challenge. The connection between computers is made by wiring the machines together; the process by which these network connections are made is virtually invisible to the user.

The same process becomes noticeably more complicated when the users in question are salespeople based in the field. The most obvious difference, of course, is the fact that no physical connection is possible; the connection to the network must be made over telephone lines through the use of a high-speed modem. As a result, the salesperson in the field, unlike his or her office-based counterpart, cannot stay connected to the network all day. Instead, he or she must log on when the connection is required and log off when finished. While this does not make the process insurmountably difficult, it does, at least, make it more visible to the user.

For our purposes, then, the issue is twofold. First of all, how well does a particular sales force automation software package support the sharing of information on a network (regardless of whether the salesperson is based in the office or in the field)? Second, how is the additional capability of remote access from the field supported? For the most part, software programs that can answer the first question satisfactorily can also perform adequately with regard to the second question. This is not always the case, however, so you ought to make certain that you ask both questions when you research different software packages.

Once you have been able to ascertain that a particular software package has the basic ability to function on a network, it then becomes necessary to look at the more sophisticated issue of data distribution.

Data Distribution and Synchronization

The related concepts of data distribution and data synchronization are probably the two most sophisticated concepts that we will discuss. In order to make them as clear as possible, let's take a look at a few hypothetical scenarios that have to do with how a database containing client information is handled.

In the first scenario, consider the case of Kelly, an independent manufacturer's representative. She is a classic case of a one-person operation. In this situation, the client database belongs solely to Kelly and exists on her notebook computer. Since this is a one-person operation, there is no one else who needs to have a copy of Kelly's database. Therefore, any additions or changes made to the database need not be duplicated elsewhere. Any PIM or contact manager can accommodate this level of functionality. Obviously, this scenario reflects the simplest possible situation. Of course, if your requirements were this simple, you probably would not be reading this book!

In our second scenario, Scott is one of three field-based salespeople working for Acme Widgets, a small manufacturer. Scott and his counterparts report to Acme's sales manager who is based at headquarters. The company keeps a master customer listing on its file server at headquarters.

Since it would be unwieldy and impractical for Scott to maintain a copy of the entire master listing on his notebook computer, he instead keeps a file that includes only his customers. He makes changes to this file each day as he calls on customers, corresponds with customers, or adds new customers. When Scott makes his daily dial-in connection to Acme headquarters, the updated records of Scott's customers are then transmitted via modem to the master file, replacing the old records that exist there.

Scott's counterparts, of course, follow the same procedure. The movement of information between the field and Acme looks something like Figure 12-1.

In this scenario, each salesperson is working with a database that is a subset of the master database. This scenario illustrates the concept of a *distributed database*. This concept can be implemented in relatively simple ways, or it can be extremely sophisticated.

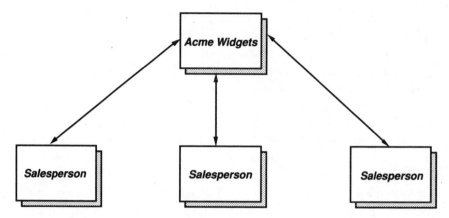

Figure 12-1. Straightforward Information Flow. The information flow requirements of a small company can be fairly simple.

For example, what would this scenario look like if Acme had a much larger sales force and field-based sales managers? Something like Figure 12-2.

Here, we can see that the information is distributed on two levels. First of all, each salesperson has access to his or her own customer records. In addition, though, all the field-based sales manager have access to the customer records of their respective salespeople. All the while, of course, a master customer file is maintained at headquarters.

If Acme's salespeople had national account responsibilities, then another level of sophistication would need to be achieved. Consider the situation that would result if our friend Scott was the account manager for Ajax Federal, a large customer with four branch offices around the country. Scott's responsibilities might include calling on the Ajax headquarters location and negotiating the prices at which all of the Ajax branch offices can buy Acme products. However, the customer requires that each Ajax branch office have its own Acme representative for ordering and customer service. The result of this requirement is that, in addition to Scott, there are four Acme account managers that call on Ajax. The challenge, from an account management standpoint, is clear. In order to properly service the customer, Scott and his manager need to know what is going on in the branch offices.

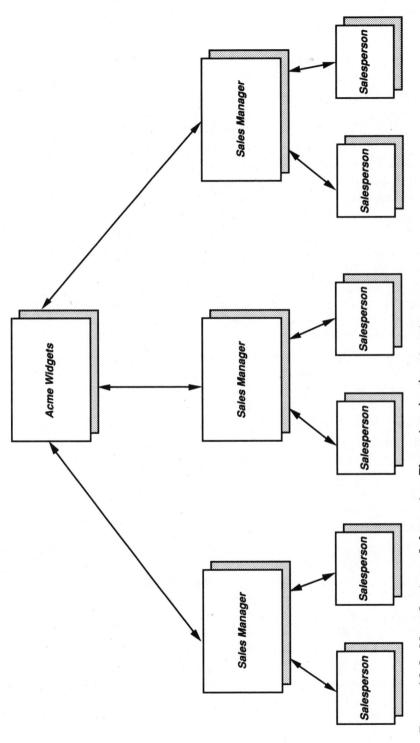

Figure 12-2. More Intricate Information Flow. As sales departments grow, the requirements for distributing information become more sophisticated.

This is a complex arrangement, but not an uncommon one. If we diagrammed the flow of information, it would look like Figure 12-3.

Five salespeople and five sales managers all need to have access to information in an appropriate manner. In addition, Acme headquarters will want a comprehensive record of everything that takes place with the account.

For all but the smallest sales groups, the ability to manage a distributed database is an essential feature for any sales force automation software that you might consider. It is the means through which everyone in the sales department can have access to all the information that is necessary to do his or her job, but not more than is appropriate for reasons of confidentiality and security.

As complex as it can be to distribute the data, managing the flow of information to the appropriate destinations is not the only challenge that this situation presents. What happens if Scott and one of his colleagues both make changes that affect a particular Ajax branch location at the same time? In such a situation, it is necessary that neither set of changes gets lost in the updating process. Instead, everyone involved ought to ultimately wind up with complete records that reflect all of the changes made. The process of reconciling the changes made to a distributed database is known as *data synchronization.*

Most sophisticated sales force automation software addresses the issue of data synchronization. Some small companies will find, though, that their sales automation requirements can be met by a software product that does not include data synchronization capabilities. Those companies can choose among several excellent software utilities available that will synchronize files created by other software packages. This solution, while not necessarily as elegant, can be more than adequate in many instances.

Your analysis of your sales force automation requirements will give you a handle on how sophisticated your needs are in the areas of data distribution and data synchronization, which can have a tremendous impact on the effectiveness of your automation project.

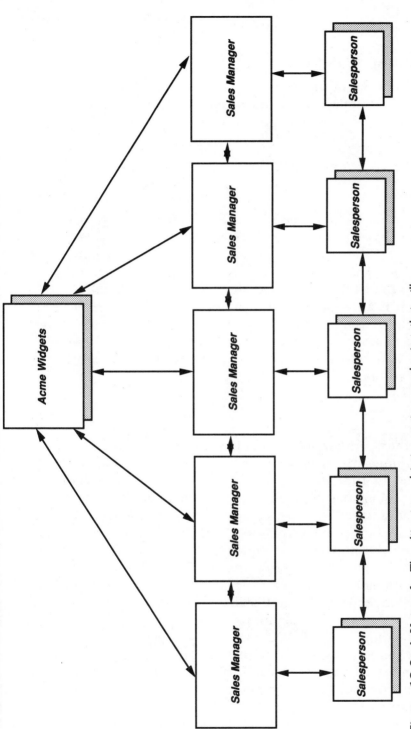

Figure 12-3. A Network. The ultimate goal is to create a mechanism that will deliver information instantly and effortlessly to wherever it is needed, in a format in which it is useful.

Operating Systems

Over 95 percent of the sales force automation software packages on the market today run on one of the three major software platforms:

1. DOS
2. Windows
3. Macintosh

While your decision to purchase a particular software package should be based primarily on the merits of that package, the platform on which the package runs can be an important consideration as well. Each of these platforms has advantages and disadvantages that will have repercussions for your automation project, so it is appropriate to review the alternatives here. This is not intended as a comprehensive discussion of the relative merits of these platforms, but it should, at least, give you some insight into the impact that your decision in this area will have relative to sales force automation.

DOS

DOS is the operating system that IBM-compatible computers use. Its beginnings date back to the introduction of the IBM personal computer in 1981. In the intervening years, it has undergone major revisions that have enhanced its capability and allowed it to take advantage of advances in hardware technology.

Unlike Windows and Macintosh, DOS is a character-based environment. The practical consequence of this is the fact that far fewer of the computer's "resources" are devoted to the creation and manipulation of screen images. As a result, programs that operate under DOS are noticeably faster than programs that operate in the other two platforms.

Another advantage of DOS is that, for the same reason, it generally requires a less fully equipped computer to run, specifically less memory and a smaller hard-disk drive. This can allow for a marginal cost savings in equipping a sales force with notebook computers.

On the other hand, DOS-based programs have generally been

found to be more difficult to learn and use. As a result, training and support costs can be measurably higher. Also, if a large segment of your sales force finds your software difficult to use, you run the risk of the entire project being undermined through poor compliance.

Perhaps more important, though, is the fact that many in the computer industry regard DOS as a platform that has an extremely limited future. While a large portion of the sales force automation products on the market are DOS-based, there is a considerable risk that your investment in DOS-based software could quickly become obsolete.

Windows

Windows is an operating environment that allows users of IBM-compatible computers to control their machines by using a pointing device (a mouse or a trackball) in conjunction with pictures (icons) and menus that appear on the computer screen. (The use of icons is the most obvious characteristic of a *graphical user interface,* or GUI. This term refers to any environment where the computer is controlled primarily by the manipulation of images on the computer screen rather than by issuing commands.) Because Windows eliminates most of the need for the user to type commands into the computer, it is considered to be much easier to learn and to use than DOS.

> I have had minor problems with the Windows package that I use, and occasionally some serious ones. But the fact of the matter is that it would be very difficult for me to go back to a DOS screen now. Once you get used to working in Windows, it is very difficult to go back.
>
> JOSEPH DE PIETRO
> *Northwestern Mutual*

Windows is also considered to be the environment of the future for IBM-compatible computers. An increasingly large share of software development is being done for the Windows environment. Similarly, many corporate users are adopting Windows as an in-house standard for their software. This decision is driven by end-user preference as well as by support costs that are lower because the software that runs under Windows is easier to use.

> A year ago, when we exhibited at trade shows, our Windows version was almost regarded as a curiosity. When we went back to that same show just recently, I don't think we showed our DOS version at all. Customers didn't want to see anything that wasn't Windows.
>
> *Sales Force Automation Software Vendor*

The fact that Windows programs can sometimes operate more slowly than DOS or Macintosh programs is a disadvantage. In addition, in order for a computer to run a Windows program, it must have more memory and a larger hard disk than it would need to run a comparably capable DOS-based program. It will also need a mouse, trackball, or other pointing device, also adding to the overall cost of the system.

Macintosh

Apple's Macintosh gave the computer world its first widely accepted graphical user interface in 1984. Since that time, Macintosh has enhanced its usability and its power simultaneously, setting the standard against which all graphical user interfaces are judged.

The Macintosh system is extremely easy to learn and to use, much more so than DOS, and, many would argue, more than Windows. Training and support costs for Macintosh systems, as a result, have been demonstrated to be much lower. In addition, because the Macintosh user interface is built in as part of the computer's basic design, its "fit and finish" is noticeably better than Windows. Macintosh hardware and software are tightly integrated to make the user's experience as productive as possible.

A commonly cited disadvantage to Macintosh systems is that they are not IBM-compatible. While it is true that data moves back and forth between Macintosh and IBM-type systems more easily than ever before, there are still some situations in which the compatibility issue can be meaningful, primarily in instances where there is the need to use particular software that is company- or industry-specific. In addition, in contrast to the tremendous number of DOS- and Windows-based programs, there are relatively fewer Macintosh-based sales force automation software packages from which to choose.

There are no hard-and-fast rules for deciding among these three alternatives. Keep in mind, though, that it is the capability of the sales force automation software itself that you should be considering. While the operating environment is important, it will usually not be the sole basis for your decision. There are extremely capable software products, at all levels of functionality, that run in each of these environments.

It is also worth noting that many sales force automation software vendors have written their software so that the information can be shared by versions of the package running in different environments. *SPS* by Saratoga Systems, for example, will accommodate DOS and Windows versions of their program running on one network using the same underlying database. This type of arrangement allows for maximum flexibility in meeting a user's needs.

Hardware Options

Your hardware decisions will be driven, for the most part, by your software decisions. DOS- and Windows-based software will run on IBM-compatible computers; Macintosh software will operate Macintosh computers. In either case, here are some of the factors that you should consider.

Color

While color can add significantly to the cost of a system, you should also consider that fact that color is more than just a cosmetic enhancement. It can also enhance a computer system's usability.

Also, if computer-based presentations are one of the applications that are important to you, then a color screen is virtually indispensable.

Size and Portability

In notebook computers, the smaller the system, the better—up to a certain point. A system can become so small that the keyboard is difficult to use, or the screen is difficult to read. For some sales force automation applications, this might be a worthwhile trade-off. If there is little need for keyboard input, then the usability of the keyboard can be sacrificed. On the other hand, if the system will be used to generate correspondence, then a somewhat larger system with a full-sized keyboard would be preferable.

> At one point, we thought about giving each salesperson a spare battery and a charger. Ultimately, we decided that was just more crap to carry around. We decided not to make them deal with any more than was absolutely necessary. Our whole package weighs less than 13 pounds. That is more than enough for anyone to carry around.
>
> DAN KLUFAS
> *Condé Nast Publications*

In general, the entire system that you supply to your salespeople should be as small and lightweight as possible, while preserving usability factors.

Docking Stations

Perhaps you have seen stereo systems that allow the cassette player to be removed and used as a Walkman. Docking stations basically do the same thing with notebook computers. When the salesperson is at the office, his or her notebook computer can be seated in a docking station. This connects the computer to a large-screen color monitor, a full-sized keyboard, and, perhaps, to the office's local area network. When the salesperson leaves the office, the notebook computer simply pops out and is ready to go.

A docking station can be a reasonable investment that allows salespeople who are in and out of the office the functionality of a full-featured desktop computer and the portability of a notebook. The Macintosh *Duo Systems* are a particularly elegant implementation of this concept.

Modems

Remember that you pay for a modem only once, but your telecommunications costs go on forever. These costs include not only long distance charges, but also the cost of your salespeople's time. This being the case, unless your communications needs are extremely modest, it will be cost effective for you to invest in the fastest modem possible. Like other areas of computer technology, modem prices have dropped dramatically in recent months, so the additional investment for a high-speed modem will not be an obstacle.

Summary

There are several levels of capability and functionality that are available in the various sales force automation software packages on the market. Moreover, these products have varying levels of capability with regard to the ability to distribute and synchronize data among various users. In this chapter, we looked at guidelines that can help you match the capabilities of a software product to the requirements of your company.

13

Implementing Your System without Stress

As we noted in Chapter 2, every company has its own approach to sales, a kind of operational fingerprint. This is one of the reasons that automation has been so long in coming to the sales department. The unique nature of every sales effort makes it virtually impossible to establish a cookie cutter approach to sales force automation. However, in the course of interviewing dozens of managers who have been very successful in their automation efforts, I have identified several fundamentals. These basic principles work in companies that are large and small, in companies that have written their own systems from scratch as well as in companies that have used packaged software, in companies whose salespeople are all in one office as well as in companies with salespeople all over the world. These basic principles are the secrets to implementing your sales force automation system without stress:

- Involve the sales force early
- Give the sales department responsibility for the system

- Use prototypes and simulations
- Make the system easy to learn and simple to use
- Automate selectively
- Provide training and support

Involve the Sales Force Early

In interview after interview, managers who had implemented successful sales force automation systems described a process of getting their salespeople involved in the project at the earliest possible opportunity. These companies began "selling" the system even before it was designed, positioning it as a tool to enhance productivity (and, therefore, income) rather than as a tool to achieve a greater degree of management control. These companies found that the early involvement of the salespeople created several advantages.

> The most important thing is to get the people involved at the beginning of the project. I would highly recommend that anybody thinking about doing this should get people involved all the way from the lowest level to senior sales management. You really should be selling the concept internally, and you have to sell it to all the people involved in the sales process. If you do not get these people involved, you are dead.
>
> RON MENZEL
> *Holmes Protection*

First of all, it allowed time for salespeople to become accustomed to the idea that the use of computers was going to become a part of their jobs. It also allowed for the identification of salespeople who had computer expertise and could, therefore, play an active role in the project. Finally, and most important, it gave management the opportunity to use the salespeople's expertise in designing the system. This last point bears further discussion.

A sales force automation system will be successful only if sales-people use it regularly and consistently. And, as we saw in Chapter 12, salespeople will not use a sales system simply because management has mandated that they do so. They will only use it if they perceive that it can help them to become more produc-tive, more effective, or more efficient. In other words, they will only use the automation system if they believe that it will enhance their ability to sell and to earn.

What many companies that have been successful with sales force automation have discovered is that the best way to gain acceptance and support among salespeople is to give them an opportunity to provide input into the design of the system. These companies have discovered that salespeople who have been involved in the process develop a feeling of ownership towards the system and, therefore, perceive themselves as having a vested interest in the ultimate success of the system. At the same time, those salespeople who cannot be directly involved in the design of the system are more receptive to a system that they know has been designed according to input from their colleagues in the field.

In any organization, if you talk to the salespeople, they will tell you what they need. They will tell you what feature they need and what capabilities they need to have. That's tremendously valuable information. Salespeople will always express their opinion. On the other hand, MIS guys will sometimes go way off in left field. Salespeople want something that can perform basic functions well. And it's got to be easy to use.

AL SMITH
Saratoga Systems

Even more important to remember: Salespeople know where the leverage points are in the sales process and, as a result, they understand where automation can impact their performance. In contrast, when management gets involved in designing sales automation systems, there is a tendency to focus on issues of reporting and system security. The folks in information systems, despite the best of intentions, tend to design systems that are technically sophisticated and functionally comprehensive, but not necessarily easy to learn or to use. The salespeople are in the best position to tell you how the system needs to work.

> We formed a task force that was made up of account managers from across the country, area managers, and some administrative people. They were all field people with a few technical guys acting as facilitators. This approach really sold upper management on the project, because they knew there was a real team of people telling what they wanted.
>
> GARY ENGEL
> *John Fluke Manufacturing Company*

Give the Sales Department Responsibility for the System

Among the companies that I studied, the most successful sales automation systems were those that were designed and "owned" by the sales department. This was generally accomplished by giving responsibility for the sales automation project to a senior sales executive—with support from MIS—rather than to the information services department.

> A key to success is to allow a much bigger piece of the design process to be actually done in the sales department.
>
> WARREN MACFARLAND
> *Harvard Business School*

The companies that adhered to this policy found it to be an indispensable aid to maintaining the focus of the project. Companies that allowed their sales force automation efforts to be driven by an MIS perspective rather than a sales perspective often found it necessary to revise the system extensively after it had been rolled out into the field. Or, as was the case with two of the companies that I studied, it was necessary to dismantle the system that MIS had created and build a new system from scratch. Needless to say, that sort of backtracking is expensive.

> I'm glad we did not put in all the bells and whistles to begin with. Because by now we'd be taking them out to put in something else.
>
> MARY ANN AMOROSA
> *Goodyear Tire and Rubber*

Use Prototypes and Simulations

The concept of giving ownership of a sales force automation project to the sales department is one of those ideas that looks fine on paper but, in the real world, presents its own set of problems. In most companies, there is no one in the sales department who has any experience that is even remotely applicable to a software development project. Without that experience, then, it is difficult to identify a process that will deliver the desired end result.

In addition, most salespeople, if asked what they would like to see in a sales force automation system, would be hard pressed to come up with ideas in an area that is so far removed from the areas of their day-to-day expertise. They would find it difficult to contribute to the project in a meaningful way.

Many companies have found that these problems can be addressed through the use of prototypes, simulations, and trial implementations. This approach can be effective for companies that develop their own systems, as well as companies that decide to purchase commercially available sales force automation software.

Storage Technology, one of the companies that was profiled earlier, made particularly effective use of this principle. Storage Technology decided to develop its own proprietary sales force automation system. Storage Technology chose Apple's Macintosh PowerBook computer as the hardware platform on which the system would run.

All Macintosh computers run a program called HyperCard. HyperCard is a Swiss army knife type of software package. It is a software package that can easily be made to perform many different functions, but it does not necessarily excel in any of them, at least not from a performance standpoint. However, the ease with which HyperCard could create computer screen designs made it an ideal prototyping tool for Storage Technology. HyperCard was used to quickly, easily, and inexpensively design all the screens for Storage Technology's sales system. When the initial set of screens was designed (and the underlying functions described), the system was shown to salespeople. The screens and the flow of the system were then reviewed and suggestions for improvement were made. This process went through several iterations until Storage Technology had a design that its salespeople felt was effective. After the design was finalized, the system was sent out to Anderson Consulting, which wrote the final system based on the design that came from the sales staff.

Another approach, used by companies who decided to buy commercially available software, is to make a small investment in an inexpensive contact manager package. That package is then used by the salespeople during a trial period. The program is not thought of as a permanent solution; instead, it becomes the basis for suggestions and refinements that define the criteria for the final software product selection.

Make the System Easy to Learn and Simple to Use

We have already seen that a sales automation system cannot be successful unless salespeople use it regularly and consistently. How easy the system is to learn and to use will have a significant impact on how extensively it is used by salespeople in the field. Therefore, companies that have been successful in automating the sales department have paid a great deal of attention to these issues.

One of the factors that makes a system easy to learn is the extent to which it harmonizes with the manual systems that are already in place. If you have a manual lead-tracking system in place, the automated system should be as similar to it as possible. The computer screen should reproduce the look of the paper forms that were used in your manual system. Even if the computer screen cannot be made to look similar, it ought to use the same language as your manual system (at least at the outset) and track the same pieces of information. Making your automated system seem familiar to your salespeople will make it less threatening and more comfortable.

We did not try to make changes on all fronts at once. We replaced the salespeople's manual functions and forms with computer screens that were very similar. This allowed them to not get sidetracked or distracted by the new system. They could concentrate on the functions they were trying to accomplish. We were not interested in trying to redefine their jobs.

DAN KLUFAS
Condé Nast Publications

As we discussed earlier, I believe that a graphical user interface can make a significant difference in how easy a system is to learn and use. In this way, even DOS-based systems, which are harder to learn than Windows or Macintosh, can take advantage of design principles that will make the system easier.

Where the rubber meets the road, though, is when you find out if the salespeople will actually use the system. And the answer to that has not nearly as much to do with the technical capability of the system as it does with user interface. It is really an art form. We sweat over every keystroke.

AL SMITH
Saratoga Systems

One of the basic design principles is the skillful use of menus to guide the salesperson through choices. Every computer screen should be constructed in a way that makes the user's options apparent and readily discernible. The user should never have to wonder, "What do I do next?"

Another principle that will make your system easier to learn is context sensitive on-line help. If a salesperson is stuck somewhere in the system and is not sure what to do next, he or she ought to be able to hit a help key to access a screen that will provide guidance for the user on how to accomplish the task at hand.

One last design principle that I will mention here is that the computer screen ought to be simple, straightforward, and free from clutter. Too many options or too much going on at one time can be daunting even for an experienced computer user. A cluttered, busy computer screen will cause technophobic salespeople to recoil in horror, bolstering their conviction that they will never be able to master this thing.

Automate Selectively

Sales force automation is a process rather than an event. Therefore, it is not necessary to automate every nook and cranny of the sales department at once. Most of the companies that have been successful in automating their salespeople have done so by using pilot projects and being selective in their automation of functions.

Use Pilot Projects

It is usually a good idea to test your sales force automation system with a small group of salespeople before rolling it out to the entire sales staff. This will allow you to make certain that you are delivering a system that is as error free as possible and optimized to function properly in your particular business environment. In addition, a pilot program will give you the opportunity to create some success stories that will be useful to you later on when it is time to roll out the system to the entire sales staff.

In deciding who ought to be included in this pilot group, there are three key factors that you will want to consider:

1. Computer experience
2. Representativeness
3. Environmental factors

Computer Experience.   In constructing your pilot program, you should look for salespeople and sales managers who are comfortable with computer technology. This will be advantageous in several ways:

- Salespeople who are comfortable with computers will be more receptive to the advantages of automation.
- These salespeople will also be less resistant to the concept of computer technology and less likely to perceive it as an intrusion.
- When ironing out any bugs or glitches in the system, computer savvy salespeople will be more helpful in identifying the source of problems.
- These salespeople will be better able to suggest ways in which the system can be made more effective.
- Participation in this type of pilot project is less likely to interfere with the productivity of computer literate salespeople.

Representativeness.   In areas other than computer experience, your pilot group should be representative of your overall sales force. This will help ensure that their experiences in testing the system will translate into a smooth and trouble-free rollout of the system to the larger sales staff.

> The two districts that we used in our pilot were selected to reflect a representative cross section of our entire sales force. We had a mixture of veteran salespeople and less experienced salespeople. Also, we made certain that there was stable management in each district to provide some continuity.
>
> GEORGE ZORBAS
> *Lederle Labs*

The pilot group ought to be calling on the same types of accounts as the rest of the sales staff. It should also have the same degree of geographic distribution as the rest of the sales staff. Finally, the pilot group ought to encompass people who are representative of the rest of the salespeople in your company with regard to level of seniority and experience in your industry.

Environmental Factors.   Finally, in choosing your pilot group, you will want to be sure that there are no factors that might mitigate against the success of the pilot project or otherwise prove to be distracting. For example, if a salesperson is in the final stages of negotiation for a large and complex order, that individual would not be a suitable candidate to participate in a pilot project. Similarly, if a sales territory has just been restructured, the salespeople involved might not be suitable for this type of project.

Of course, it would be ideal to be able to identify a totally representative group of salespeople who also happened to have a high degree of computer experience. In the real world, it is unlikely that you will be fortunate enough to do this. What, then, are the appropriate trade-offs?

When you designate your pilot group, representativeness is more important than computer experience. A pilot group that is assembled on this basis might take a little longer to get familiar with the new system, but the results will be of more value to the company when the project is finished. In the event that your pilot group does include salespeople with little computer experience, the process will be easier if the sales manager involved can supply some computer background. (Many of the managers that I spoke with were initially concerned about finding people with computer experience. They were surprised to find that a large number of their salespeople and sales managers actually had computers at home.)

Select Initial Functions

In addition to the use of a pilot group involving selected salespeople, many of the companies that were successful with sales force automation chose to automate a limited number of tasks or functions at the outset of their automation project. Only after this initial automation effort was implemented and the new methodology was assimilated by the salespeople did these companies seek to expand the areas in which they made use of automation technology.

A common starting point was the use of electronic mail to facilitate communications between the home office and the field. Electronic mail can be fairly straightforward, so it is not a difficult application for most salespeople to learn. In addition, in those companies that had a field-based sales force, this type of communication almost always represented an area in which computer technology could be introduced easily and to great advantage.

Other companies found that the use of an intelligent electronic catalog, replacing cumbersome three-ring binders, was the best place to start. Whatever the starting point was, though, the principle was the same: Create momentum by getting the salespeople comfortable with using computer technology in specific areas. Then, after they have achieved some productivity gains, begin to automate other functions. With this approach, we see again that sales force automation is a process rather than an event.

Provide Training and Support

If there is one single area where we can separate the winners from the losers, it is in the area of training and support. Without exception, the companies that were successful in automating their sales departments were committed to training their people on how to use the system properly and to supporting their salespeople in the field.

> The development of these tools is not enough. Proper training and assimilation are the crucial issues. Making these systems effective is more a game of implementation than it is of vision. In other words, figuring out what to do is only about 15 percent of the job. Actually making it happen accounts for the other 85 percent.
>
> WARREN MACFARLAND
> *Harvard Business School*

In some instances, these companies brought the salespeople to headquarters to be trained. In other instances, the training was done in the field. Where and how the training took place was of less importance than the fact that each successful company made sure that every single salesperson knew how to use the system properly. And in every case, the prevailing attitude from management was that it was the company's responsibility to make sure that the training was adequate; in no case was the responsibility for learning the system placed primarily in the salespeople.

The philosophy of this project is that if there is a problem, it is never the user's fault. We have tried to make the system as foolproof as possible.

DAN KLUFAS
Condé Nast Publications

Some clever and innovative ideas in the area of training came from Condé Nast, the magazine publisher. For the benefit of salespeople who were unfamiliar with computers, Condé Nast included a game with the system, so that the salespeople could get used to the system in a completely nonthreatening environment. In addition, Condé Nast included with their system a tutorial program on how to type, so that salespeople could practice their keyboard skills!

In addition to training, all of the companies I studied had made provisions for field-support of salespeople who had problems with the system or questions about its use. In some instances, the company had one or two people dedicated to supporting the salespeople in the field. They were available to answer questions and help diagnose problems. In other instances, cooperative support arrangements were made with the software vendors. In every case, though, the salespeople knew that there was someone to call if there was a problem or a question.

As important as training is the availability of people to provide support for people in the field, usually by telephone. People need to be able to call in and say, "I am doing this. Why isn't it working?" We do this with an in-house help desk. Salespeople can call in with a problem, and they get walked through the process to resolve the problem.

RON MENZEL
Holmes Protection

Summary

While every sales force automation scenario is different, every successful installation had these elements in common:

- The sales force was involved early in the process
- Sales department was given responsibility for the system
- The system was built for the salespeople, not for management
- Prototypes and simulations were used
- The system was made easy to learn and to use
- Sales functions were selectively automated
- Attention was given to training and support

PART 5
Horizons

14

Get Ready for the Future

Bill Clinton's theme song during his 1992 presidential campaign was "Don't stop thinking about tomorrow." Those words represent a valuable piece of advice for sales managers who are starting to dip their toes in the invigorating waters of sales force automation technology. As was noted at the outset of this book, sales force automation is no longer a competitive advantage; it is a competitive necessity in the hypercompetitive business climate of the 1990s. However, sales managers who are beginning to look at the possibilities that sales force automation can create for their organizations should keep in mind that this technology is very much a moving target. Technological advances are occurring regularly, and at breathtaking speed.

While it is true that some advances can safely be ignored as being merely technology for its own sake, it is also important to note that there are several new technologies on the horizon that hold the promise of real productivity gains for the sales force. In this chapter, we are going to look at four areas of emerging technologies that will certainly make a significant difference in the field of sales force automation in the decade to come. Each of these technologies is in its infancy and must mature before becoming widely useful. But each has the potential to generate tremendous gains in productivity for the companies that can employ it creatively. The four areas that we are going to explore are:

1. Pen-based computing and personal digital assistants
2. Wireless communications
3. Collaborative computing (groupware)
4. Artificial intelligence and expert systems

Pen-Based Computing and Personal Digital Assistants

Even though notebook computers have gotten smaller and, as a result, more convenient to use, there are still some sales situations in which notebook computers will never be appropriate. The restrictions are seldom technical.

In some instances, they are cultural. For example, while interviewing a customer or prospect, a salesperson will often make notes on a legal pad or in a spiral-bound notebook. I believe that regardless of how ubiquitous sales force automation becomes, it will never be appropriate to flip up the screen of a notebook computer and start entering notes on the keyboard while conducting a conversation with a customer. If a salesperson attempted to do so, the conversation would be disrupted. In such a situation, sales automation technology would be intruding on the sales process rather than supporting it.

There are other instances when the use of a notebook style computer would simply be physically inconvenient. For example, some salespeople, because of the nature of the products they sell and the accounts they call on, must write up their orders while they are walking or standing. They cannot do this with a traditional notebook computer. The size of the machine is not the problem in these situations. The problem is that with only two hands, it is almost impossible for salespeople to simultaneously stand up or walk, hold their computer, and use the keyboard.

Both of these problems can be addressed through the use of pen-based computers. (See Figure 14-1.) These systems are generally about the same size and weight as notebook computers, usually about six or seven pounds. In addition they have the same amount of computing "horsepower" as their notebook-style counterparts. Pen-based computers do not have a keyboard; instead, a stylus or pen is the computer input device. The user writes on the computer screen with the pen just as he or she would write on a paper pad, using it instead of the keyboard to enter information. Certain manufacturers, notably Grid Systems, are experimenting with designs that incorporate both a keyboard and a pen, allowing the user to switch between the two input devices, as appropriate.

A pen-based system allows a salesperson sitting in front of a

Figure 14-1. Pen-Based Computers. There are many sales situations in which using a keyboard would be inconvenient or inappropriate. Pen-based systems will be more functional; they will also be acceptable to use in many business situations where a keyboard would not. *(Courtesy of Fujitsu.)*

client to take notes during the conversation. The form of the computer makes this no more intrusive than it would be for that same salesperson to take notes using a pad or notebook. Also, this type of hand-held computer can be used by a salesperson who is walking or standing, perhaps filling in quantities on an electronic order form. In either scenario, pen-based computers would greatly increase the number of situations in which sales force automation technology could be applied.

The technological breakthroughs necessary to make pen-based systems usable and affordable have proved to be somewhat more elusive than was originally forecast by pen proponents. Creating technology to allow the computer to reliably recognize pen input of any sort has turned out to be a tricky proposition. In addition, there is still much work to be done in the area of handwriting recognition. Of course, there are many possible ways in which salespeople could use a pen-based computer that would not be dependent on the computer's ability to recognize handwriting. However, most computer industry observers agree that this piece of the technological puzzle must be in place before pen-based systems move into the mainstream of the computer marketplace.

Pen-based computing will be a tremendous advance in the world of computers in general, and in the field of sales force automation in particular. None of the technical issues that remain to be addressed appears to be insurmountable. As a result, I predict that pen-based computers will move into the mainstream of the computer world very quickly. Sales force automation software that is specifically designed to take advantage of the unique capabilities of pen-based systems is already being developed. As you think out the long-term automation strategy for your sales department, you should keep an eye on this technology, and consider the aspects of your sales operation in which it could possibly be useful.

Pen-based computing solutions are likely to become mainstream in the relatively near future. Slightly further off on the horizon is the widespread use of personal digital assistants, or PDAs. PDAs are hand-held computing and communications devices that are not much larger than standard calculators. (See Figure 14-2.) While they are less powerful than pen-based computers, their smaller size and form makes them more convenient

Figure 14-2. Personal Digital Assistants. Personal digital assistants hold a great deal of promise for a not-too-distant future. Today, however, manufacturers are still searching for the right combination of price, form, and function. *(Courtesy of Apple Computers, Inc. Dave Martinez, photographer.)*

to carry and use. While Sharp and Casio have been marketing forerunners of PDA-type devices for several years, this category was launched in earnest by Apple Computer with the recent introduction of its extraordinary Newton Message Pad. Just as Macintosh represented a breakthrough in making desktop computers easier to learn and use, Newton has created the same sort of breakthrough in the PDA arena, creating a legitimacy for these devices that had previously not existed.

The most important difference between pen-based computers and PDAs is that the former are essentially evolutionary variations of the desktop and notebook computer technologies that we have been using for years, whereas the latter are based entirely on new technology. As a result, we can assume that PDAs will not have the same diversity of software as their pen-based cousins for some time.

The future of PDAs as mainstream, industrial strength sales tools is bright, albeit distant. It is likely that they will evolve into superintelligent communications tools that also act as information management devices. To the extent that they can communicate with the home office and put information in the hands of your salespeople, they will certainly have a place in your long-term sales automation plans. However, it will be some time before these products can offer real day-to-day usefulness. Even though PDAs are new, sleek, and sexy, as a sales manager, your immediate attention should remain focused on other, more immediately usable technologies.

Cellular and Wireless Communications

It was not the size of laptop and notebook computers that made them a meaningful technological breakthrough. Rather, it was the fact that they were battery-operated and, therefore, allowed users to work in places like automobiles and airplanes, where a power cord was not conveniently accessible. Toward the end of the 1980s, salespeople who had begun to explore the productivity enhancements of technology were liberated from the confines of the office and empowered to use their computers in the field.

Contact management was the most common application of sales force automation. As sales departments expanded the ways in which they use computer technology, the aspect of sharing information, distributing it between the office and the field, became more and more important.

However, just as the mobility of sales technology was once hampered by the need to be able to plug into an outlet, the communications capabilities of current sale technologies is constrained by the need to be able to plug into a telephone line. New technologies are emerging that promise to eliminate the last barriers that prevent your salespeople from being in touch with the office from virtually anywhere. (See Figure 14-3.) Different technologies provide different capabilities, but the end result is that communication will be less constrained than ever before.

A wide variety of wireless communications technologies are currently competing for prominence in the world of mobile computing. Some of the most promising contenders on the technological horizon include:

- Cellular—The same technology that drives cellular phones can transmit data, as well. Many vendors currently offer cellular modems.

- Packet radio—The technology that is utilized in paging devices can be used to transmit and receive electronic mail. Motorola's EMBARC is an example of this technology.

- Packet cellular—Competing proposals exist to make use of existing cellular structures to deliver digital packet messages.

Each of these technologies has its own strengths and weaknesses, advantages and disadvantages. A comprehensive discussion of each is beyond the scope of this book, but there are several important points that deserve your attention.

First of all, for the reasons described above, you should keep in mind the fact that as wireless communication technologies mature, they are certain to become important enough and powerful enough to be the centerpiece of many sales managers' automation strategies.

Also be mindful of the fact that, as you survey various options, you will find that the appropriate choice of wireless technology

Figure 14-3. Always in Touch. Technology is developing the capability to allow mobile sales professionals to phone, fax, or share data at anytime, from anywhere. *(Courtesy of Eo.)*

will depend largely on the nature of your communications requirements. Interactive communications have far different requirements and constraints than merely sending and receiving data. Each sales situation will, as was noted in Chapter 11, have its own imperatives and leverage points. These will drive your technology choices.

Finally, it should be noted that the widespread adoption of wireless technologies will only happen over a long period of time, far longer than industry proponents would like to believe. The reasons for this are bureaucratic more than technical. The federal government and, to a lesser extent, state governments have regulatory control over the ultimate disposition of the questions that surround wireless technology. As a result, the final determinations about how wireless technologies are implemented are not likely to be made anytime soon.

In the end, though, wireless communications technologies will have a powerful impact on the way that field-based sales operations are run.

Collaborative Computing (Groupware)

The image of the field-based salesperson as a lone warrior, out by himself on the competitive battleground is a romantic one. But like so many romantic images, it is severely out of date and bears little relationship to the current business reality. The fact of the matter is that in the 1990s, successful salespeople must exhibit the ability to work in teams. In order to provide the level of service that today's customers demand, salespeople must interact and collaborate with other salespeople as well as colleagues in other departments of the company. Today's business environment finds salespeople more involved with other areas of the company than ever before. The "You make it, we'll sell it" approach is an artifact of the distant past. Salespeople increasingly find themselves in the role of conduit between customer, manufacturing, and research and development. Moreover, large corporate customers are demanding that they be serviced by a team that is coordinated among various branch locations.

Throughout this book, we have examined the use of computer technology to support the sales effort. The conceptual model of most software is oriented towards a single user. As network and communications technologies have become more sophisticated, the conceptual model of software has evolved to include the ability to move information around as well as the ability to consolidate information from many users at a management level.

The next logical step in this evolution is software that is built from the ground up around the premise of people joined together and working together through a computer network. In fact, such software has already begun to appear on the market. *Notes* from Lotus Development is widely regarded to be the early standard in this category and, as this is being written, commands an overwhelming share of the "groupware" market.

Notes acts as a framework around which companies can develop software applications that facilitate group productivity (in contrast with traditional software which is designed to enhance individual productivity). It would be accurate to think of *Notes* as a development environment for groupware applications, much as dBase was once the standard development environment for database applications.

Groupware represents a major paradigm shift in the world of computers. As a result, it is certain to proceed with the fits and starts that are common to any brand-new approach. But as the collaborative skills of our salespeople become more and more important in the new selling environment of the 1990s, it is clear that new software tools will be necessary to reflect this change.

Artificial Intelligence and Expert Systems

Salespeople, like other professionals, operate under various sets of rules. These rules sometimes relate to the products that are being sold. For example, if Widget A needs Gizmo B in order to function properly, we expect our salespeople to be familiar with that requirement and to construct sales orders accordingly. The salesperson's ability to do this not only enhances customer service, but it also lowers costs since a correctly completed sales order does not need to be reentered and reshipped. Other rules under which salespeople operate can relate to various other aspects of the sales function, including:

- Anticipated sales order cycles
- Follow-up procedures
- Adjusting product mix for maximum profit

All of these sets of rules can be incorporated into software that seems to act as an "expert" assistant to the salesperson, or an *expert system.* This type of software program is also sometimes said to exhibit *artificial intelligence,* a term that is widely used but is somewhat too broad, in my judgment, to be really useful.

Expert systems can be expensive to develop and difficult to integrate into the real-world selling environment. However, as the systems become widely incorporated into sales operations, they will provide several benefits. Expert systems will:

- Reduce costs (as noted above)
- Reduce training expenses, allowing new salespeople to become productive more quickly
- Enhance profitability by assuring the most advantageous product mix
- Enhance customer service by eliminating unnecessary mistakes
- Improve close ratios by monitoring the progress of each customer's sales cycle

Although larger corporations with ample resources are already experimenting with expert systems in the sales department, it will be quite a while before they become a mainstream product that is available to most sales departments. But, like other aspects of sales force automation, expert systems will, no doubt, ultimately become widely implemented. The productivity payback that they promise is too great to assume otherwise.

Appendix A

Sales Force Automation Software Vendors

Abend Associates
265 Winn Street
Burlington, MA 01803-2616
(800) 288-5383
Fax: (617) 273-3053
Platform: DOS, Windows

Advanced Concepts, Inc.
4129 N. Port Washington
Avenue
Milwaukee, WI 53212
(414) 963-0999
Fax: (414) 963-2090
Platform: DOS

Advanced Marketing Systems
190 Littleton Road
Westford, MA 01886
(508) 392-0366

Fax: (508) 392-0215
Platform: DOS, Windows

After Hours Software
Tri Center Plaza
5990 Sepulveda Blvd.
Van Nuys, CA 91411
(818) 780-2220
Fax: (818) 780-2666
Platform: Macintosh

American Business
Information
5711 So. 86th Circle
P.O. Box 27347
Omaha, NE 68127
(402) 593-4565
Fax: (402) 331-5481
Platform: DOS, Windows

Arlington Software + Systems
Corp.
56 Bartletts Island Way
Marshfield, MA 02050
(617) 837-0424
Fax: N/A
Platform: DOS, Windows

Automation Technologies
948 East 7145 South
Suite C-206
Midvale, UT 84047
(800) 777-6368
Fax: (801) 566-8559
Platform: All

Blackstone & Cullen, Inc.
2000 RiverEdge Parkway
Suite 800
Atlanta, GA 30328
(800) 828-1299
Fax: (404) 612-1470
Platform: Macintosh,
Windows

Breakthrough Productions
210 Park Avenue
Nevada City, CA 95959
(916) 265-0911
Fax: (916) 265-8036
Platform: Macintosh

Brock Control Systems, Inc.
2859 Paces Ferry Road
Suite 1000
Atlanta, GA 30339
(404) 431-1200
Fax: (404) 431-1201
Platform: DOS, Windows

Business Software, Inc.
701 San Conrado Terrace

Suite #5
Sunnyvale, CA 94086
(408) 736-3000
Fax: (408) 730-5165
Platform: Macintosh,
Windows

Campbell Services, Inc.
21700 Northwestern Highway
Suite 1070
Southfield, MI 48075
(313) 559-5955
Fax: (313) 559-1034
Platform: DOS, Windows

Cartesia Software
5 South Main Street
P.O. Box 757
Lambertville, NJ 08530
(609) 397-1611
Fax: (609) 397-5724
Platform: All

Chang Labs
10228 North Stelling Road
Cupertino, CA 95014
(408) 727-8096
Fax: (408) 252-3081
Platform: Macintosh

ClientSource Corporation
1921 Palomar Oaks Way
Suite 100
Carlsbad, CA 92008
(619) 431-7007
Fax: (619) 434-2396
Platform: DOS, Windows

CogniTech Corporation
8601 Dunwoody Place
Suite 450
Atlanta, GA 30350

(404) 518-4577
Fax: (404) 518-4588
Platform: Windows

Coker Electronics
1430 Lexington Avenue
San Mateo, CA 94402
(415) 573-5515
Fax: (415) 573-5515
Platform: DOS, Windows

Colleague Business Software
10000 Research Blvd.
Suite #210
Austin, TX 78759
(800) 926-9965
Fax: (512) 345-9965
Platform: Macintosh

Computer Solutions &
Development, Inc.
7315 Wisconsin Avenue
Suite 200 West
Bethesda, MD 20814
(301) 951-5505
Platform: DOS, Windows

Contact Software International
1840 Hutton Drive
Suite 200
Carrollton, TX 75006
(800) 365-0606
Fax: (214) 919-9760
Platform: All

CorNet Sales & Marketing
Systems
701 Main Street
Stroudsburg, PA 18360
(717) 420-0800
Fax: (717) 420-0818
Platform: All

Data Systems Support
1228 Shelly Court
Orange, CA 92668
(714) 771-0454
Fax: (714) 771-3028
Platform: Other

DataModes, Inc.
4200 Perimeter Center Drive
Suite 202
Oklahoma City, OK 73112
(405) 947-3887
Fax: (405) 947-5948
Platform: DOS, Windows

Dendrite International, Inc.
7 Powder Horn Drive
Warren, NJ 07059
(908) 271-8383
Fax: (908) 271-5144
Platform: DOS, Windows

Diamante Software
14330 Midway Road
Suite 119
Dallas, TX 75244
(214) 661-3855
Fax: (214) 661-5504
Platform: Macintosh

Digital Equipment Corporation
10 Tara Boulevard
Nashua, NH 03062
(603) 884-0807
Fax: (603) 884-2253
Platform: All

Dimensional Insight, Inc.
99 South Bedford Street
Burlington, MA 01803
(617) 229-9111
Fax: (617) 229-9113
Platform: All

Droege Computing Services,
Inc.
1816 Front Street
Suite 130
Durham, NC 27705
(919) 383-9749
Fax: (919) 382-7422
Platform: DOS

Dynacomp, Inc.
The Dynacomp Office
Building
178 Phillips Road
Webster, NY 14580
(716) 265-4040
Fax: N/A
Platform: DOS

Dynamacs, Inc.
7954 Transit Road
Suite 323
Williamsville, NY 14221
(800) 755-2616
Fax: N/A
Platform: DOS

Dynatec Systems Corporation
750 West Lake Cook Road
Suite 385
Buffalo Grove, IL 60089
(708) 808-2700
Fax: (708) 808-2714
Platform: DOS, Windows

E-Z Data, Inc.
533 South Atlantic Blvd.
Monterey Park, CA 91754
(800) 777-9188
Fax: (818) 458-9097
Platform: DOS

ELAN Software Corporation
4916 Gerald Avenue
Encino, CA 91436
(800) 654-3526
Fax: (818) 999-9872
Platform: DOS

EMIS Software, Inc.
901 NE Loop 410
Suite 526
San Antonio, TX 78209
(800) 593-8499
Fax: (512) 822-8509
Platform: DOS

ENDPOINT! Marketing
Information Systems
1230 Oakmead Parkway
Suite 210
Sunnyvale, CA 94086
(800) 488-5322
Fax: (408) 738-5979
Platform: Macintosh

Envoy Systems Corp.
400 Fifth Avenue
Waltham, MA 02154
(617) 890-1444
Fax: (617) 890 -4178
Platform: DOS

Excalibur Sources, Inc.
Box 467220
Atlanta, GA 30346
(404) 956-8373
Platform: DOS, Windows

Fairfield Management
Resources, Inc.
1051 Perimeter Drive

Suite 1175
Schaumburg, IL 60173
(708) 706-9141
Platform: DOS

Fastech, Inc.
450 Parkway Drive
Broomall, PA 19008
(215) 565-3405
Fax: (215) 544-3695
Platform: DOS

Field Integration Technology,
Inc.
4960 Almaden Expressway
Suite 327
San Jose, CA 95118
(408) 927-6404
Fax: (408) 927-6312
Platform: Macintosh

Gateway Systems Corporation
4660 South Hagadorn
Suite 110
East Lansing, MI 48823
(517) 337-8960
Fax: (517) 337-2868
Platform: DOS

GE Information Services
401 North Washington Street
Rockville, MD 20850-1785
(800) 433-3683
Fax: (301) 340-5306
Platform: All

GeoQuery Corporation
475 Alexis R. Shurman Blvd.
Suite 380E
Naperville, IL 60563-8453
(708) 357-0535

Fax: (708) 717-4254
Platform: Macintosh

GEOVISION, Inc.
5680 Peachtree Parkway
Norcross, GA 30092
(404) 448-8224
Fax: (404) 447-4525
Platform: Windows

Greenlight Software
Elan Associates Division
79 West Monroe #1320
Chicago, IL 60603-4969
(312) 782-6495
Fax: (312) 782-6494
Platform: Macintosh

Group 1 Software, Inc.
6404 Ivy Lane
Suite 500
Greenbelt, MD 20770
(800) 368-5806
Fax: (301) 982-4069
Platform: DOS

High Caliber Systems, Inc.
171 Madison Avenue
Suite 806
New York, NY 10016
(212) 684-5553
Fax: (212) 532-2362
Platform: DOS

HMS Computer Company
5937 Fairwood Drive
P.O. Box 1707
Minnetonka, MN 55345-0707
(612) 934-2652
Fax: (612) 933-9664
Platform: DOS, Macintosh

Informatics Group, Inc.
100 Shield Street
West Hartford, CT 06110
(800) 348-1377
Fax: (203) 953-7407
Platform: DOS

Information Dimensions, Inc.
5080 Tuttle Crossing
Boulevard
Dublin, OH 43017-3569
(800) DATA MGT
Fax: (614) 761-7290
Platform: Other

Information Management
Associates
6527 Main Street
Trumbull, CT 06611
(203) 261-4777
Fax: (203) 261-2516
Platform: Other

Information Science Associates
676 N. St. Clair
Suite 1880
Chicago, IL 60611
(312) 787-2723
Fax: (312) 787-2901
Platform: All

Inquiry Intelligence Systems
12842 Pennridge Drive
Bridgeton, MO 63044
(314) 298-0599
Fax: (314) 298-0995
Platform: DOS

Inquiry Plus
814 Eagle Drive
Bensenville, IL 60106
(708) 595-5059

Fax: (708) 595-5361
Platform: DOS

JEB Systems, Inc.
9 Village Circle
Suite 450
Westlake, TX 76262
(800) 821-1006
Fax: (817) 430-5870
Platform: DOS

Key Systems Inc.
1454 Cherokee Road
P.O. Box 4777
Louisville, KY 40204-0777
(800) 827-0376
Fax: (502) 473-1912
Platform: DOS

Leadtrack Corp.
620 Colonial Park Drive
Suite 100
Roswell, GA 30075
(404) 587-0412
Fax: none
Platform: All

Los Altos Software
425 First Street
Suite E
Los Altos, CA 94022
(415) 941-6030
Fax: (415) 941-9072
Platform: Other

Lotus Development
Corporation
55 Cambridge Parkway
Cambridge, MA 02142
(800) 343-5414
Fax: (617) 693-3899
Platform: All

LSW, Inc.
1801 Brightseat Road
Landover, MD 20785
(301) 772-8700
Fax: (301) 772-8722
Platform: DOS, Windows

MapInfo
200 Broadway
Troy, NY 12180
(800) 327-8627
Fax: (518) 274-6066
Platform: All

Market Power, Inc.
101 Providence Mine Road
Suite #104
Nevada City, CA 95959
(916) 265-5000
Fax: (916) 265-5171
Platform: DOS, Windows

Marketing Information
Systems, Inc.
1840 Oak Avenue
Suite 400
Evanston, IL 60201
(800) 243-3885
Fax: (708) 491-0682
Platform: All

Marketrieve Company
50 Nashua Road
Suite 108
Londonderry, NH 03053
(800) 234-6587
Fax: (603) 425-2450
Platform: All

MarketWorks, Inc.
5 Dellwood Court
San Rafael, CA 94901

(800) 627-5389
Fax: (415) 485-4327
Platform: DOS

ME-DI-CO, Inc.
2233 Northwestern Avenue
Sec. F
Waukegan, IL 60087
(708) 249-1213
Fax: (708) 249-1448
Platform: DOS

Micromega Systems, Inc.
832 Baker Street
San Francisco, CA 94115
(415) 346-4445
Fax: (415) 346-6804
Platform: DOS

Modatech Systems, Inc.
1681 Chestnut Street
4th Floor
Vancouver, BC V6J 4M6
(604) 736-9666
Fax: (604) 736-4996
Platform: DOS, Windows

National Management Systems,
Ltd.
1945 Old Gallows Road
Suite 206
Vienna, VA 22182
(703) 827-0797
Fax: (703) 790-1965
Platform: DOS

Nine to Five Software
P.O. Box 18899
Boulder, CO 80308
(800) 292-5925
Fax: (303) 443-4386
Platform: Macintosh

NPRI, Inc.
70 Mansell Court
Suite 100
Roswell, GA 30076
(404) 594-7514
Fax: (404) 998-9887
Platform: DOS, Windows

OAC, Inc.
365 Northridge Road
Suite 260
Atlanta, GA 30350
(800) 562-7638
Fax: (404) 395-0603
Platform: DOS

Paul Guggenheim & Associates,
Inc.
601 Skokie Boulevard
Northbrook, IL 60062
(708) 498-2299
Fax: (708) 498-2527
Platform: Other

PenUltimate, Inc.
19000 MacArthur Blvd.
Suite 620
Irvine, CA 92715-1444
(714) 476-6360
Fax: (714) 476-8411
Platform: Windows

Perceptive Solutions, Inc.
P.O. Box 12956
Lake Park, FL 33403
(407) 626-4561
Fax: (407) 694-6899
Platform: DOS

Performance Software, Inc.
100 Shield Street
West Hartford, CT 06110

(800) 348-1377
Fax: (203) 953-7407
Platform: DOS

PharmaSystems, Inc.
106 Headquarters Plaza
North Tower, 5th Floor
Morristown, NJ 07960-3959
(201) 993-9339
Fax: (201) 993-1192
Platform: DOS, Windows

PMI Software
733 Academy Street
Kalamazoo, MI 49007
(800) 745-1539
Fax: (616) 343-1539
Platform: DOS, Macintosh

Polaris Software, Inc.
17150 Via Del Campo
Suite 307
San Diego, CA 92127-2110
(800) PACKRAT
Fax: (619) 674-7315
Platform: Windows

Popular Programs, Inc.
6915 LaGranada
Houston, TX 77083
(713) 530-1195
Fax: (713) 530-1358
Platform: DOS, Windows

Prism Systems Inc.
P.O. Box 40968
Indianapolis, IN 46240
(317) 872-4808
Fax: (317) 257-5379
Platform: DOS

Productive Access, Inc.
21087 Carlos Road
Yorba Linda, CA 92686
(714) 693-7423
Fax: N/A
Platform: DOS, Windows

Profit Management Systems,
Inc.
9800 Fourth Street North
Suite 204
St. Petersburg, FL 33702
(800) 229-7674
Fax: (813) 578-6325
Platform: DOS

Progressive Networks, Inc.
10565 Old Placerville Road
Sacramento, CA 95827
(916) 368-7080
Fax: (916) 368-7082
Platform: DOS, Windows

Quest Management Systems,
Inc.
580 Kirts Boulevard
Suite 315
Troy, MI 48084-4138
(313) 362-3770
Fax: (313) 362-4686
Platform: DOS

Remote Control International
5928 Pascal Court
Carlsbad, CA 92008
(800) 835-MAGIC
Fax: (619) 431-4006
Platform: All

Richmond Technologies
Software, Inc.
6400 Roberts Street

Suite 420
Burnasq, BC Canada V5G 4C9
(604) 299-2121
Fax: (604) 299-6743
Platform: DOS

SaleMaker Corporation
59 Stiles Road
Salem, NH 03079
(603) 893-2422
Fax: (603) 898-4582
Platform: All

Sales Implementation Systems
20771 Catamaran Lane
Huntington Beach, CA 92646
(714) 841-1134
Fax: N/A
Platform: DOS

Sales Management Systems,
Inc.
1420 NW Gilman Blvd.
#2127
Issaquah, WA 98027
(800) 444-9945
Fax: (206) 391-0710
Platform: DOS

Sales Technologies, Inc.
3399 Peachtree Road
The Lenox Building, Suite
700
Atlanta, GA 30326
(404) 841-4000
Fax: (404) 841-4115
Platform: DOS, Windows

SalesBook Systems
1545 East Avenue
Rochester, NY 14610
(800) 336-3415

Fax: (716) 244-4284
Platform: Macintosh,
Windows

SalesKit Software Corporation
763 South New Ballas Road
St. Louis, MO 63141
(800) 779-7205
Fax: (314) 567-0439
Platform: All

SalesLink Systems
1840 Oak Avenue
Evanston, IL 60201
(708) 866-0400
Fax: (708) 866-1808
Platform: Windows

SalesMark Software, Inc.
8269 Fredericksburg Road
San Antonio, TX 78229
(800) 622-4978
Fax: (512) 614-0639
Platform: Macintosh,
Windows

SALESPRO International
229 Ward Circle
Suite A13
Brentwood, TN 37024-2008
(615) 371-1190
Fax: (615) 371-1083
Platform: DOS

Salmon Systems
700 112th Avenue NE
Bellevue, WA 98004
(206) 637-7070
Fax: (206) 451-0294
Platform: DOS, Windows

Saratoga Systems Inc.
1550 S. Bascom Avenue
#230
Campbell, CA 95008
(408) 371-9330
Fax: (408) 371-9376
Platform: DOS, Windows

Scherrer Resources, Inc.
8200-2 Flourtown Avenue
Philadelphia, PA 19118
(800) 950-0190
Fax: (215) 836-1804
Platform: DOS

Smart Software, Inc.
4 Hill Road
Belmont, MA 02178
(800) 762-7899
Fax: (617) 489-2748
Platform: DOS

SNAP Software
175 Canal Street
Manchester, NH 03101
(603) 623-5877
Fax: (603) 623-5562
Platform: DOS, Windows

Software of the Future, Inc.
P.O. Box 531650
Grand Prairie, TX 75053
(800) 766-7355
Fax: (214) 262-7338
Platform: DOS

SouthWare Innovations, Inc.
555 Stage Road
P.O. Box 3040
Auburn, AL 36831-3040
(205) 821-1108
Fax: (205) 821-1146
Platform: DOS

SPSS Inc.
444 N. Michigan Avenue
Chicago, IL 60611
(312) 329-3300
Fax: (312) 329-3668
Platform: All

Strat*x International
222 Third Street
Cambridge, MA 02142
(617) 494-8282
Fax: (617) 494-1421
Platform: DOS

Strategic Mapping, Inc.
3135 Kifer Road
Santa Clara, CA 95051
(408) 970-9600
Fax: (408) 970-9999
Platform: DOS

SuperOffice
One Cranberry Hill
Lexington, MA 02173
(617) 674-1101
Fax: (617) 674-2970
Platform: Macintosh,
Windows

Systems Management, Inc.
1011 E. Touhy Avenue
Des Plaines, IL 60018
(800) 323-1143
Fax: (708) 803-3539
Platform: Other

Tactics International Limited
16 Haverhill Street
Third Floor
Andover, MA 01810
(800) 927-7666
Fax: (508) 475-2136

Platform: Macintosh,
Windows

Target Microsystems, Inc.
1852 Blacks Road
Hebron, OH 43025
(800) 735-5776
Fax: (614) 928-2883
Platform: DOS

Televell, Inc.
1629 South Main Street
Milpitas, CA 95035
(408) 956-0511
Fax: (408) 956-0202
Platform: DOS, Windows

The August Corporation
P.O. Box 7835
Auburn, CA 95604
(916) 268-3691
Fax: (916) 268-3693
Platform: DOS

The Salinon Corporation
7424 Greenville Avenue
Suite 115
Dallas, TX 75231
(214) 692-9091
Fax: (214) 692-9095
Platform: DOS

Thoughtware, Inc.
200 South Biscayne
Boulevard, Suite 2750
P.O. Box 011151
Miami, FL 33101-1151
(305) 854-2318
Fax: (305) 374-2718
Platform: DOS

Trilogy Development Group
6034 West Courtyard Drive
Suite 130
Austin, TX 78730
(512) 794-5900
Fax: (512) 794-8900
Platform: Macintosh,
Windows

TTG, Inc.
10 State Street
Woburn, MA 01801
(617) 932-6500
Fax: (617) 932-6238
Platform: Windows

UNITRAC Software
Corporation
229 East Michigan Avenue
Kalamazoo, MI 49007
(616) 344-0220
Fax: (616) 344-2027
Platform: Windows

Vertex Software
115 Evergreen Heights Drive
Pittsburgh, PA 15229
(800) 333-4845
Fax: (412) 931-4429
Platform: DOS

Westchester Distribution
Systems, Inc.
P.O. Box 324
Scarsdale, NY 10583
(914) 723-5230
Fax: N/A
Platform: DOS

WestWare, Inc.
10148 Diamond Head Court
Spring Valley, CA 91977-5317

(800) 869-0871
Fax: (619) 660-0233
Platform: Macintosh

WindSoft, Inc.
66 Ford Road
Denville, NJ 07834
(201) 586-4400
Fax: (201) 586-9045
Platform: All

WinSales, Inc.
25018 104th Avenue S. E.
Suite C
Kent, WA 98031
(206) 854-9480
Fax: (206) 852-5434
Platform: Windows

XYZT Computer Dimensions,
Inc.
150 Broadway
Suite 1001
New York, NY 10038
(212) 608-6655
Fax: (212) 385-4831
Platform: DOS, Windows

ZS Associates
1800 Sherman Avenue
Suite 700
Evanston, IL 60201
(708) 492-3600
Fax: (708) 864-6280
Platform: Other

Appendix B

Sales Force Automation Consultants

Bentz & Associates
3778 Silverwood Drive
York, PA 17402-4355
Fax: (717) 755-8948

Business Development
Associates
590 Galer Street
Suite 111
Seattle, WA 98101
(206) 282-8418
Fax: (206) 282-8418

Clarity Systems
725 S. Catalina Avenue
Pasadena, CA 91106
(818) 568-0509
Fax: (818) 568-0032

Concepts In Sales
P.O. Box 12956
Lake Park, FL 33403
(407) 626-4561
Fax: (407) 694-6899

Contact Systems
2211 E. Winston Road
Suite K
Anaheim, CA 92806-5399
(714) 535-5078

Dream IT
1255 Cedar Ridge Lane
Colorado Springs, CO 80919
(719) 598-9000
Fax: (719) 598-9089

Information Systems
Marketing, Inc.
2950 Van Ness Street NW
Suite 110
Washington, DC 20008
(202) 363-8996
Fax: (202) 363-7667

Outlook on Mobile Computing
P.O. Box 917
Brookdale, CA 95007-0917
(408) 338-7701
Fax: (408) 338-7806

ProMark Solutions
17 Donnybrook Road
Montvale, NJ 07645
(201) 476-1863
Fax: (201) 476-1863

Research & Information
Services
1635 Mill Run Court
Lawrenceville, GA 30245
(404) 822-1668
Fax: (404) 995-7337

Sales and Marketing
Technologies
65 Fuller Lane
Hyde Park, NY 12538
(914) 229-7014

Sales Automation, Inc.
18 Heron Hill
Downingtown, PA 19335
(800) 922-5545
Fax: (215) 458-0330

Sales Software Source
566 West Adams
Suite 506

Chicago, IL 60661
(312) 258-9700
Fax: (312) 258-0616

Sales Systems International
10 Piedmont Center
Suite 904
Atlanta, GA 30305
(404) 231-5984

Software Showcase Consultants
10018 Dove Oak Court
Cupertino, CA 95014
(408) 996-8393
Fax: (408) 996-1118

Spectrum/Data One
7 Deerpark Drive
Suite E
Monmouth Junction, NJ
08852
(908) 274-3400
Fax: (980) 274-3489

The Denali Group
2815 NW Pine Cone Drive
Issaquah, WA 98027-8698
(206) 392-3514
Fax: (206) 391-7982

The IDK Group, Inc.
6101 W. Cintenella
Suite 340
Culver City, CA 90230
(800) 327-1898
Fax: (310) 348-1160

The Perera Group
20 Rowes Wharf TH3
Boston, MA 02110-3325
(617) 261-0112
Fax: (617) 261-0112

Index

About the Author

George W. Colombo is a professional speaker, writer, and consultant who heads his own sales training and automation firm, Influence Technologies. His seventeen-year career in sales and management spans a variety of industries, including thirteen years in the computer field, and he has trained hundreds of salespeople in various aspects of selling. He keeps abreast of new products and applications as a monthly columnist for a leading computer industry trade publication. An active professional speaker, Mr. Colombo also addresses audiences regularly on sales-related issues. He lives and works in Merrimack, New Hampshire.